Love

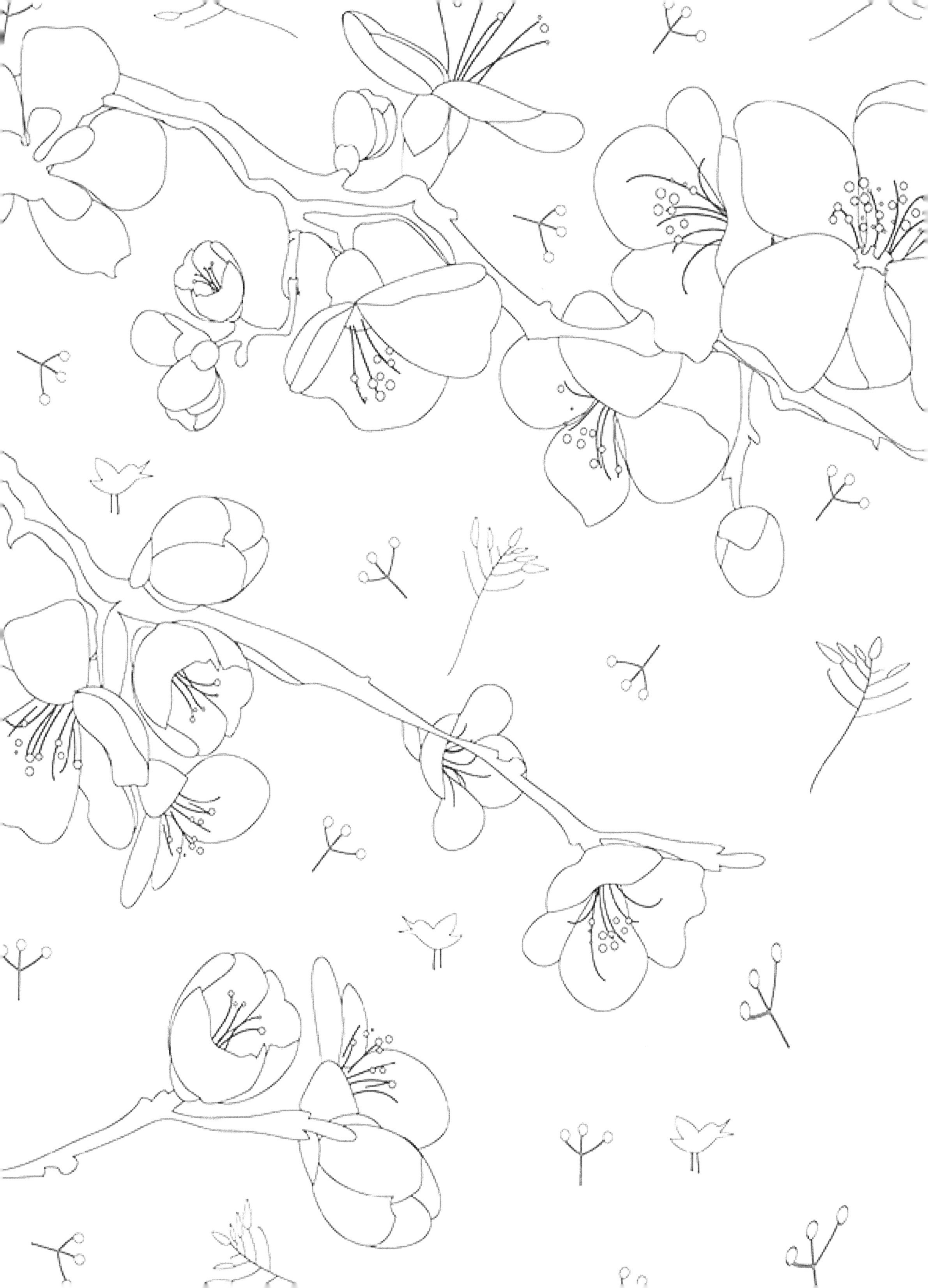

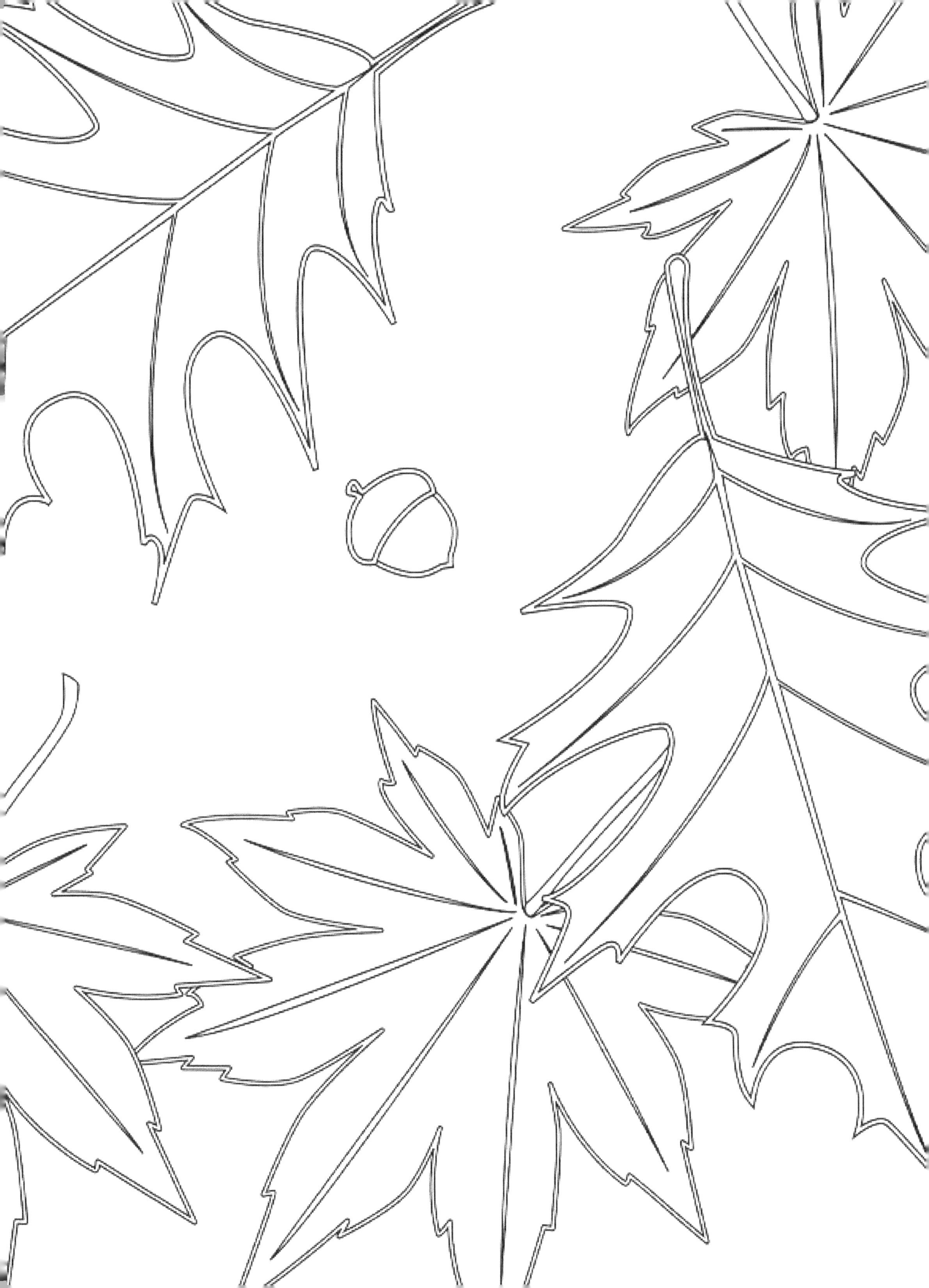

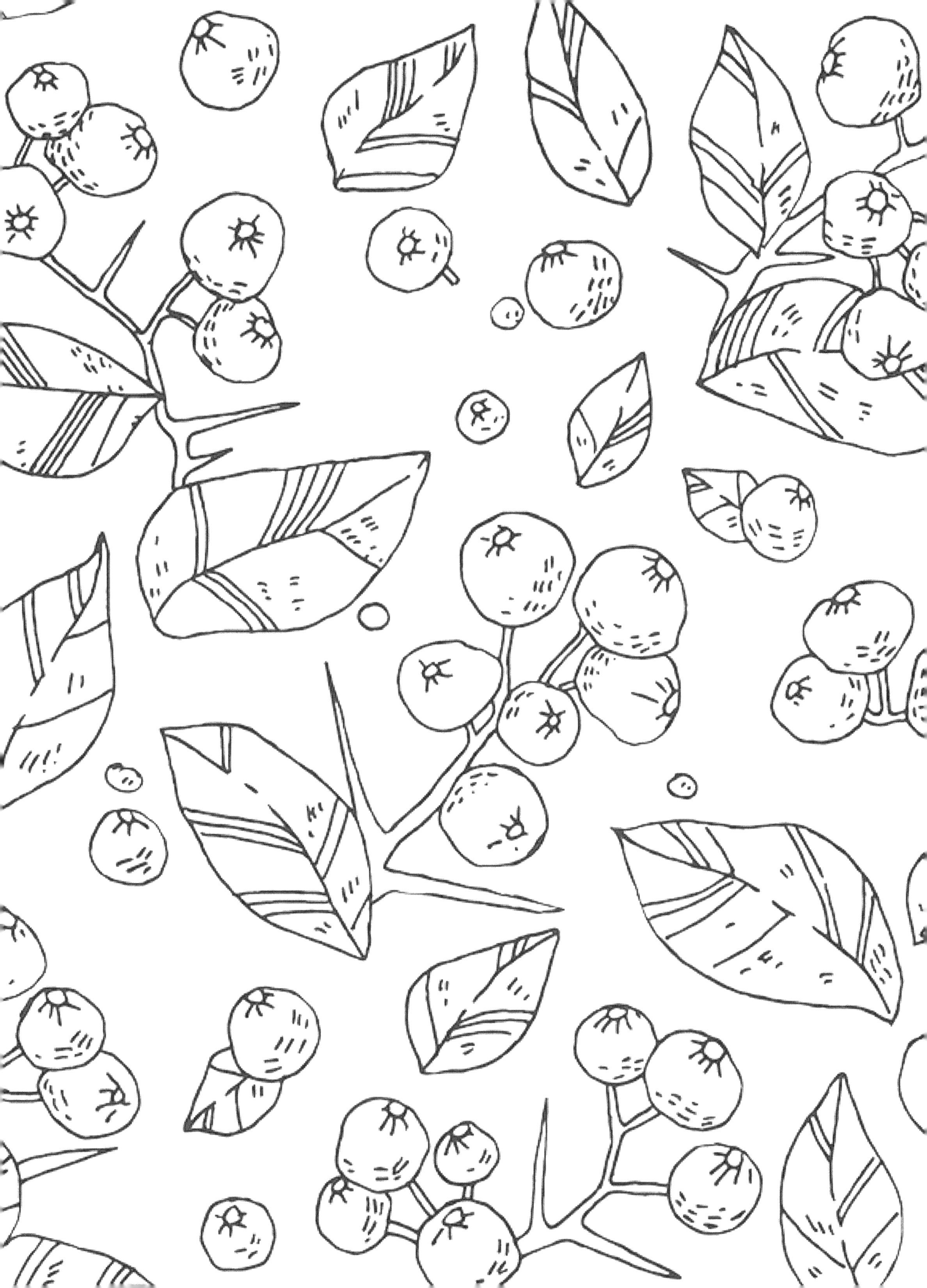

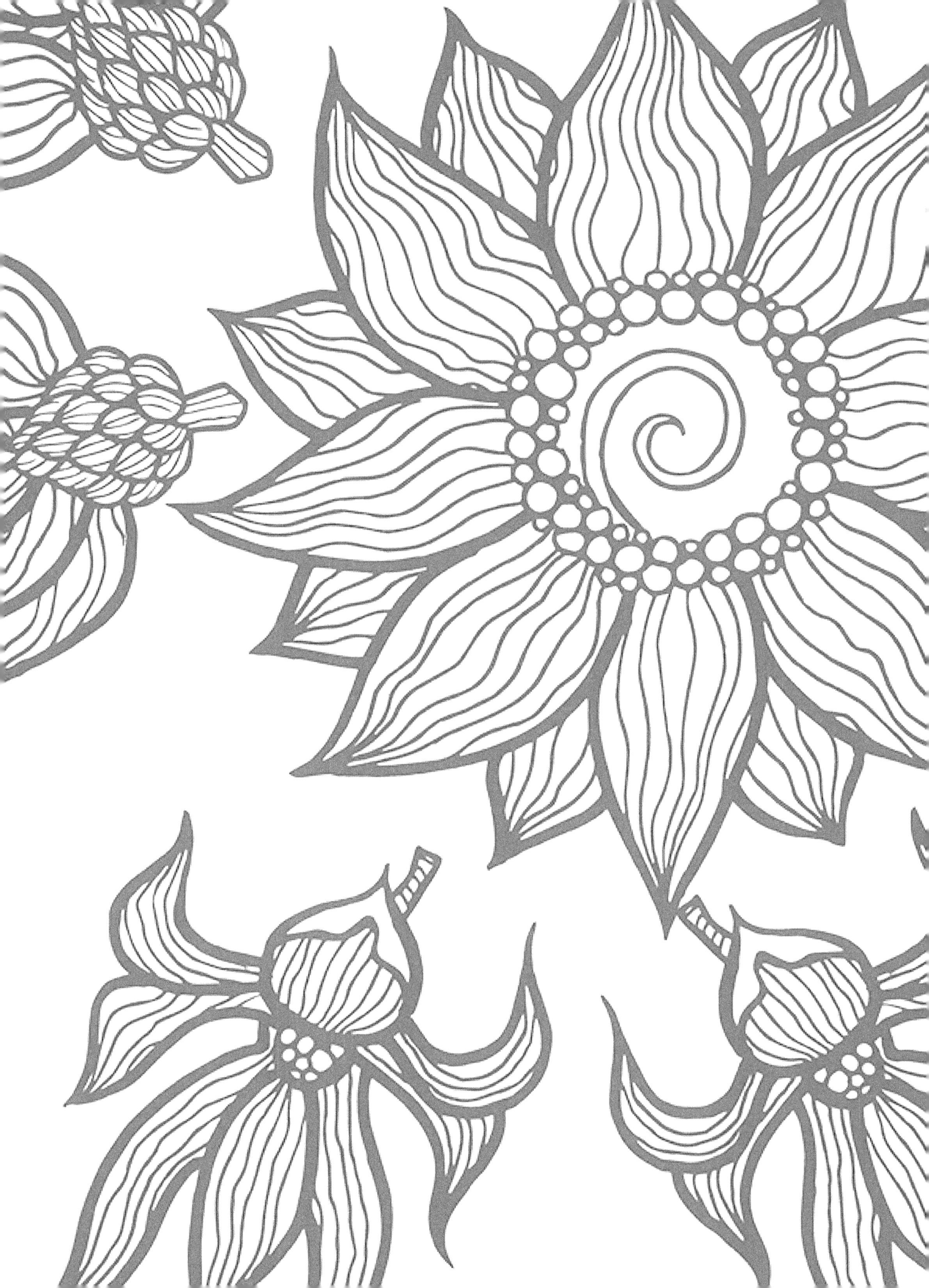

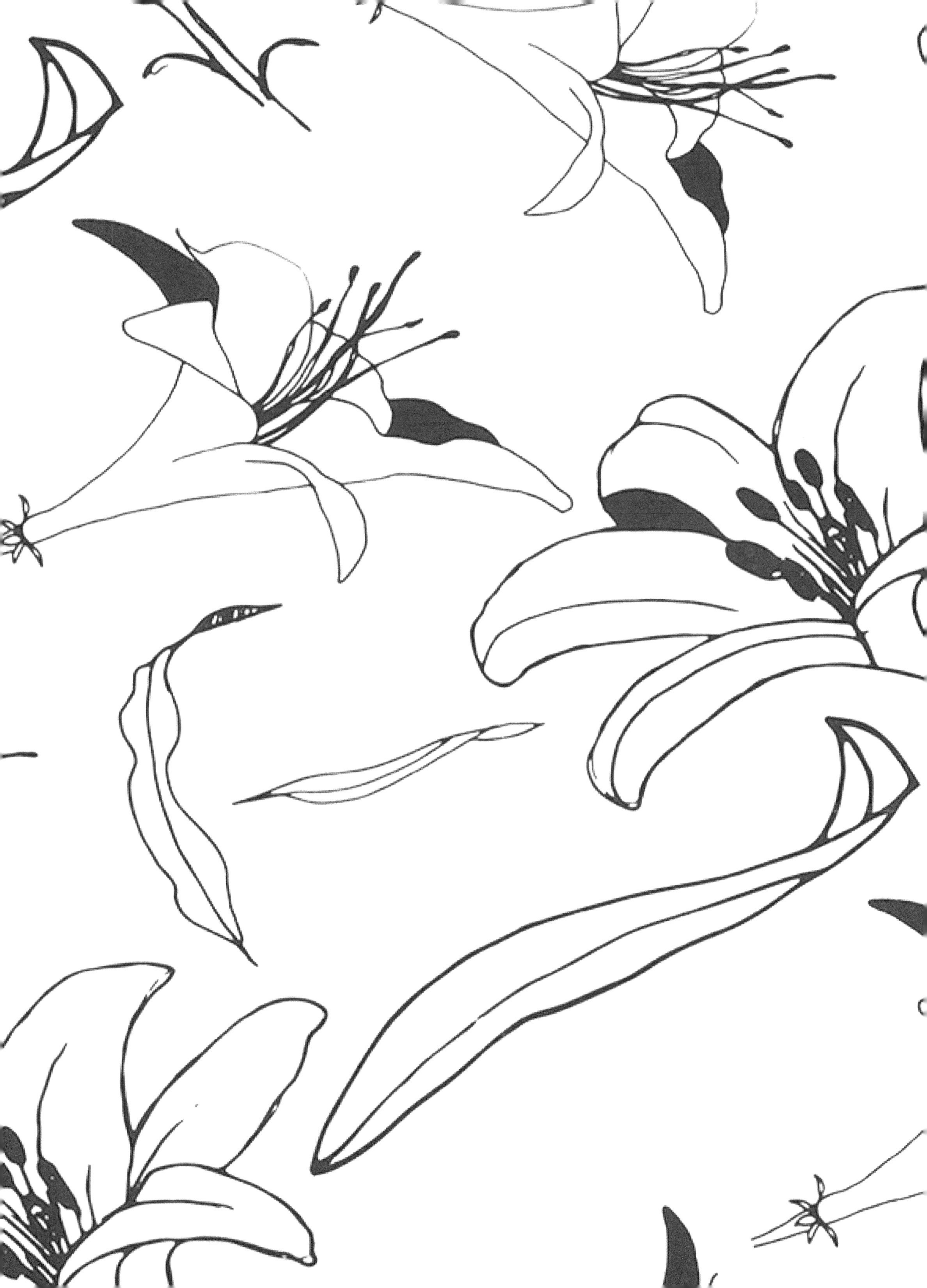

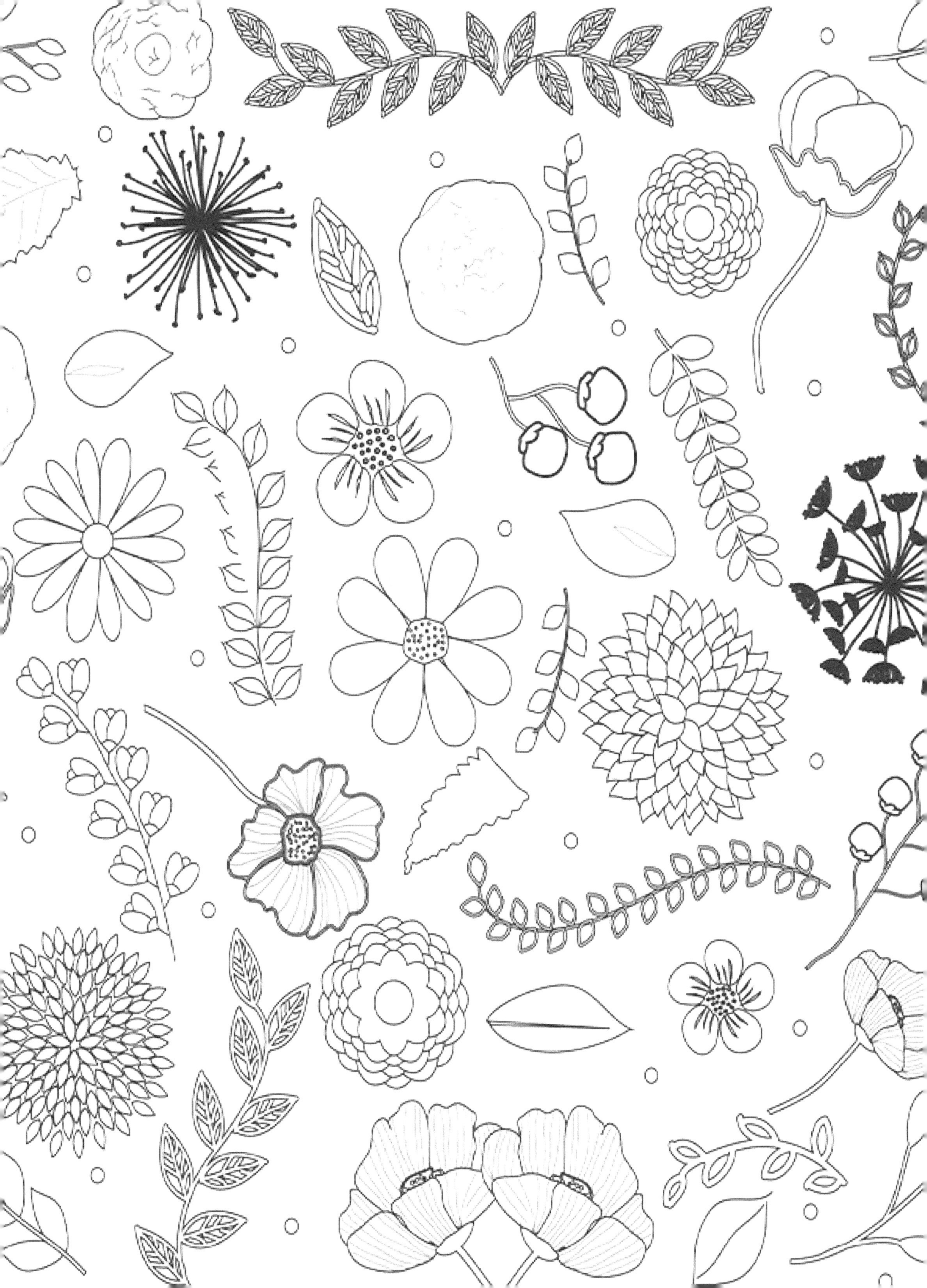

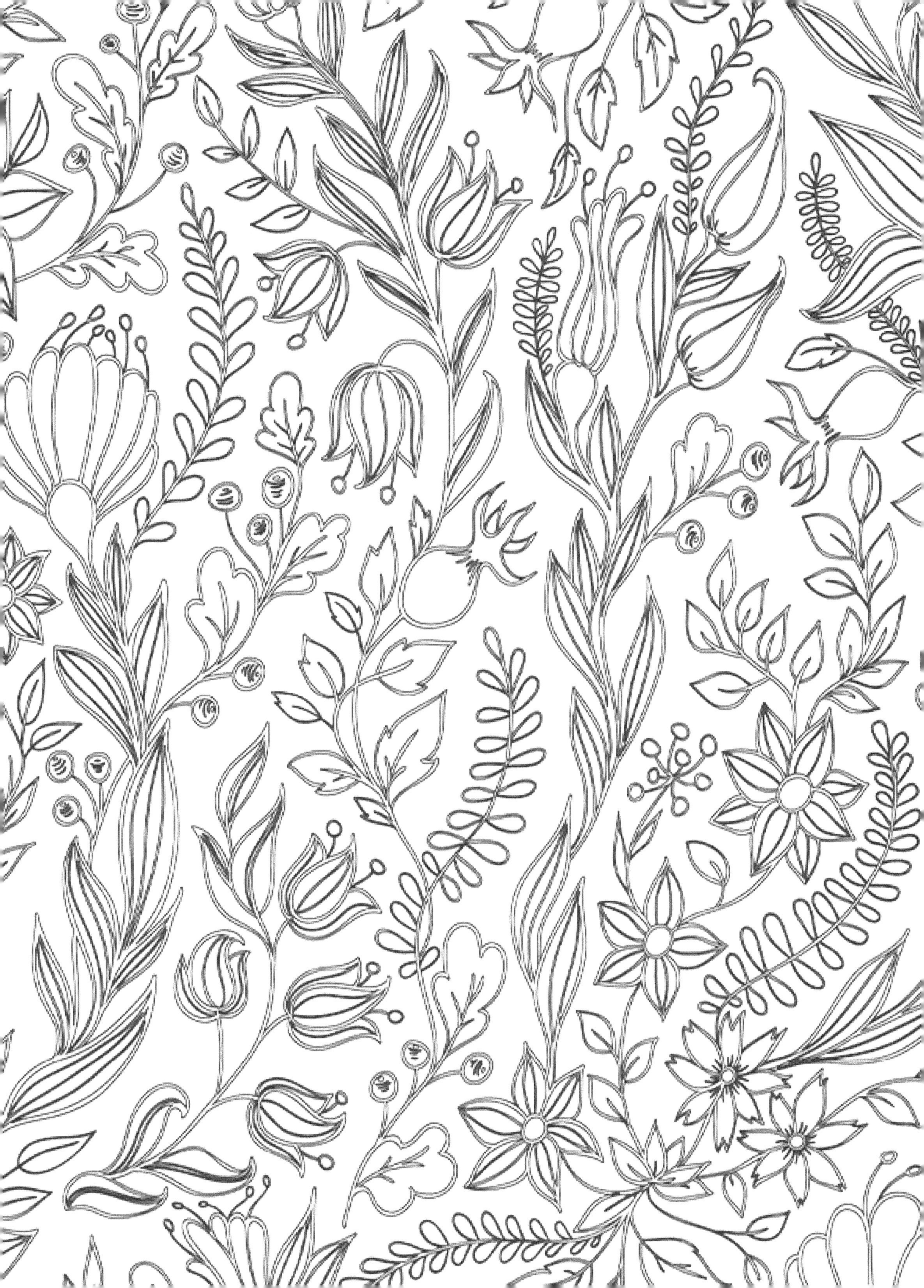

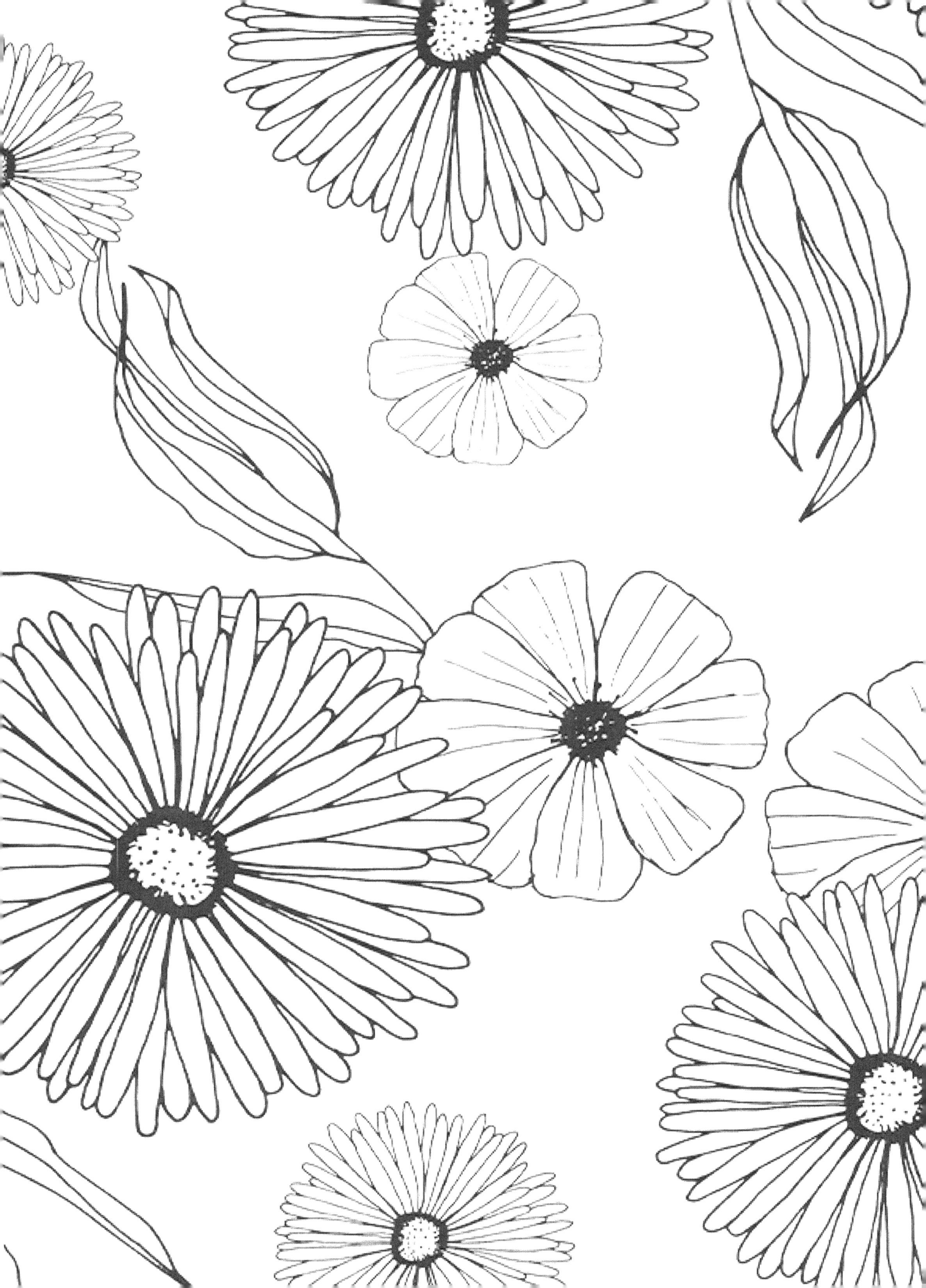

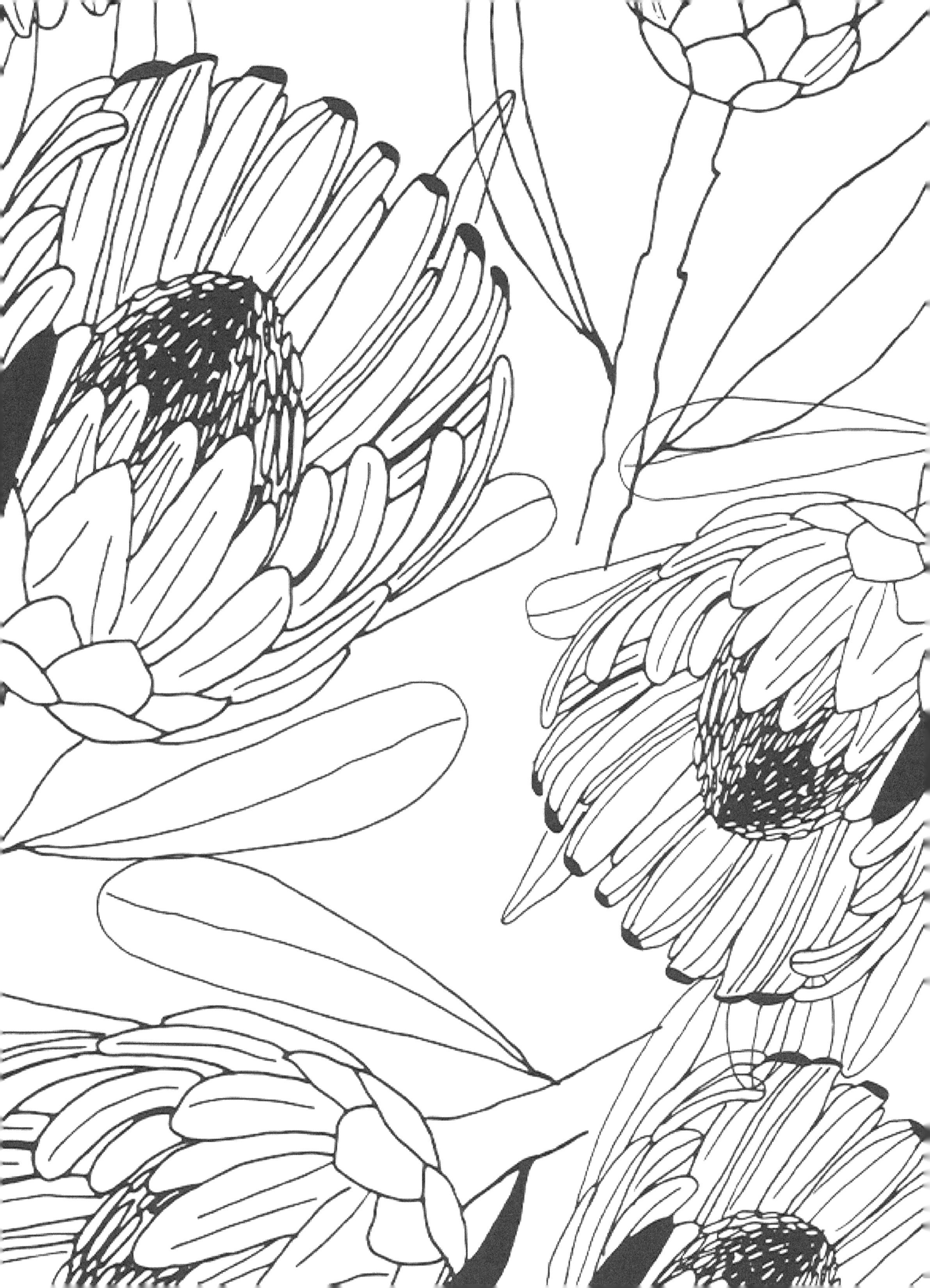

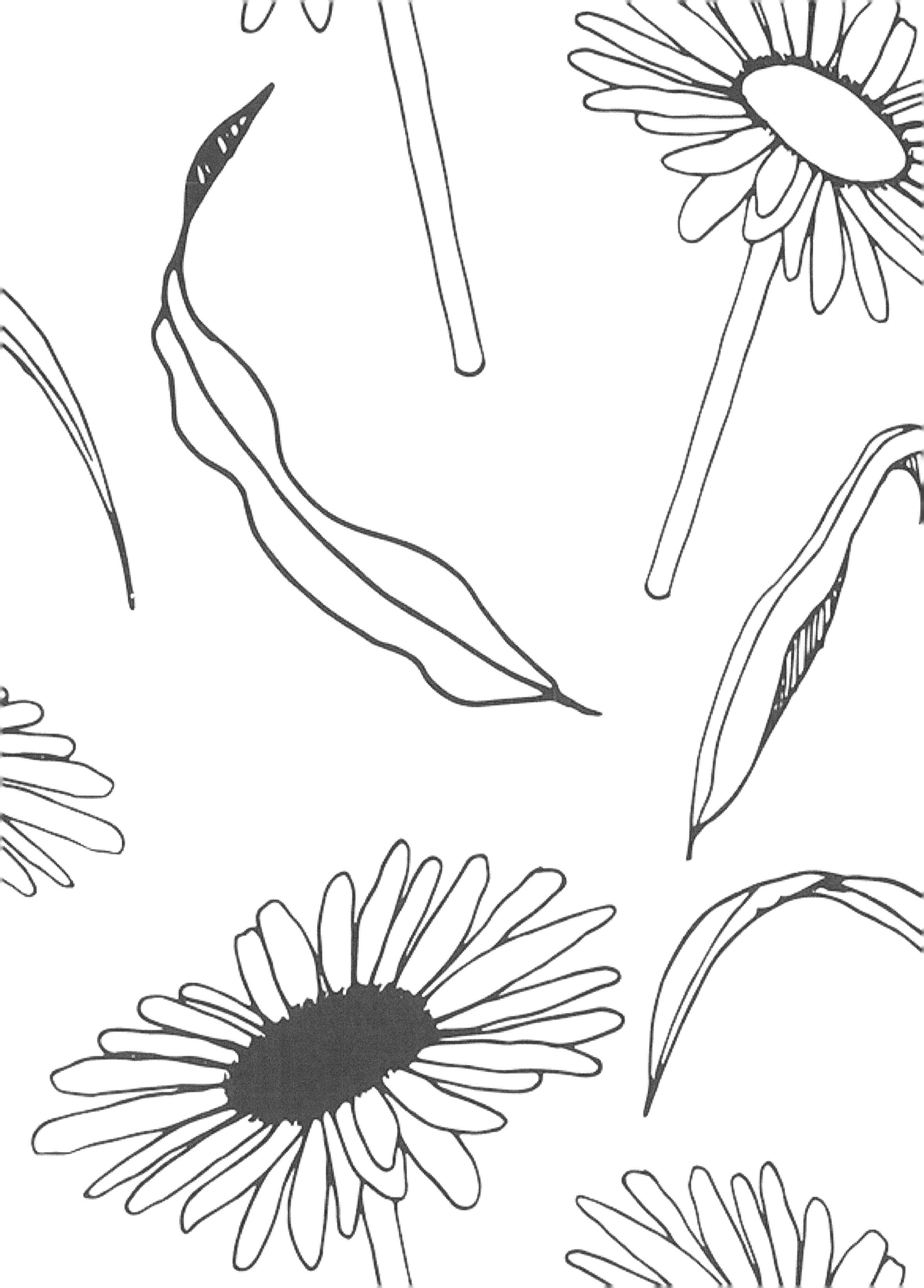

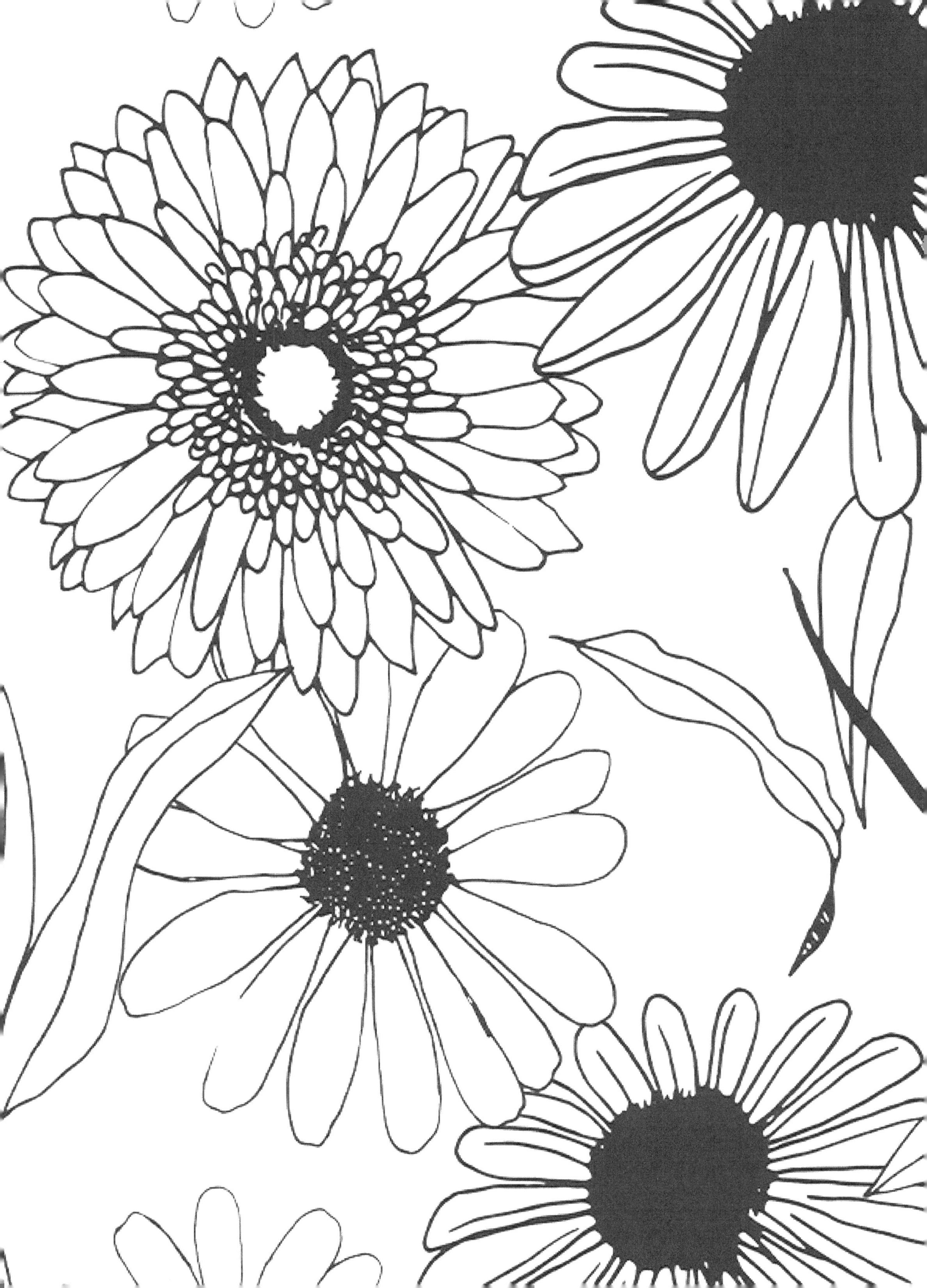

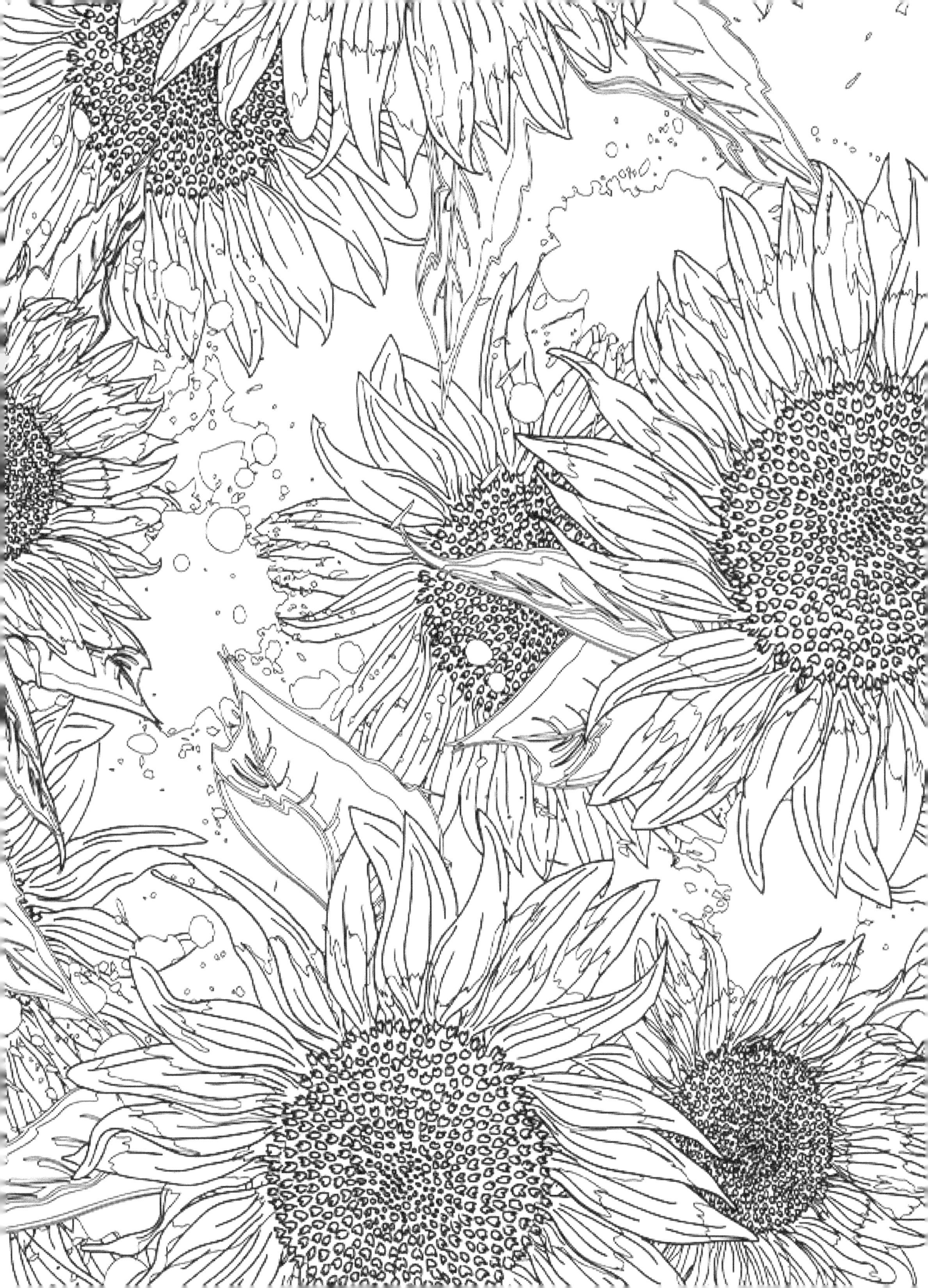

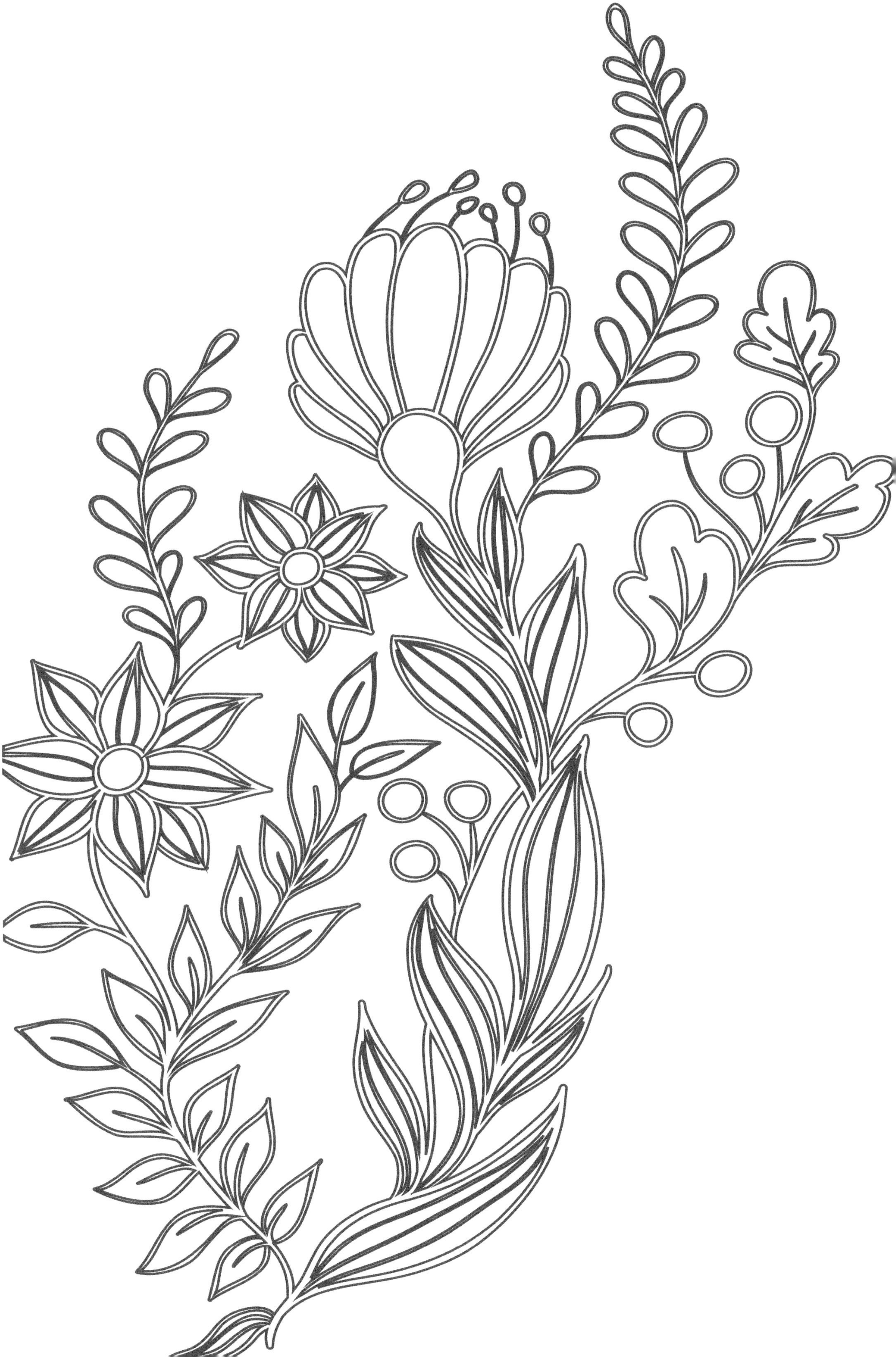

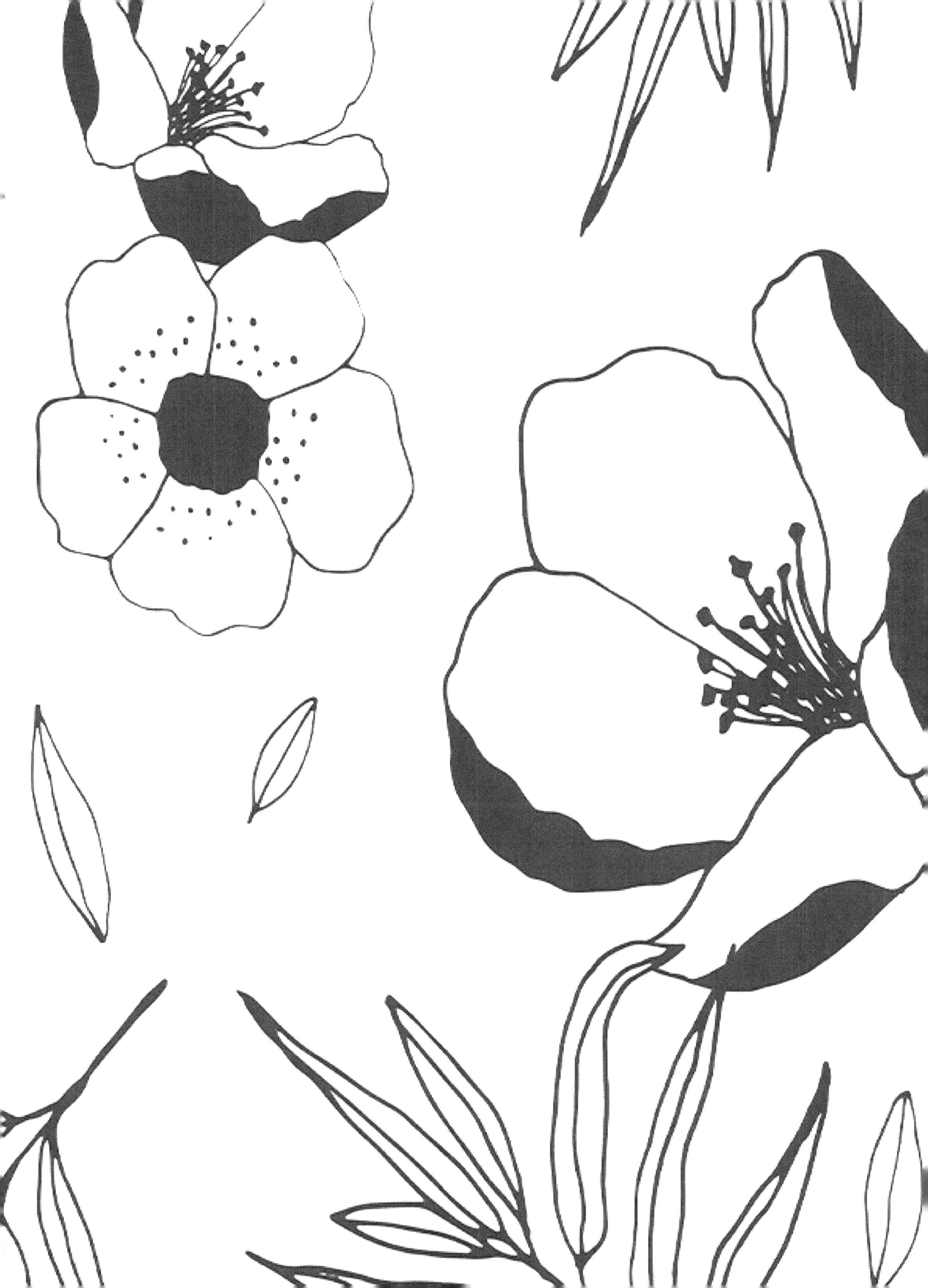

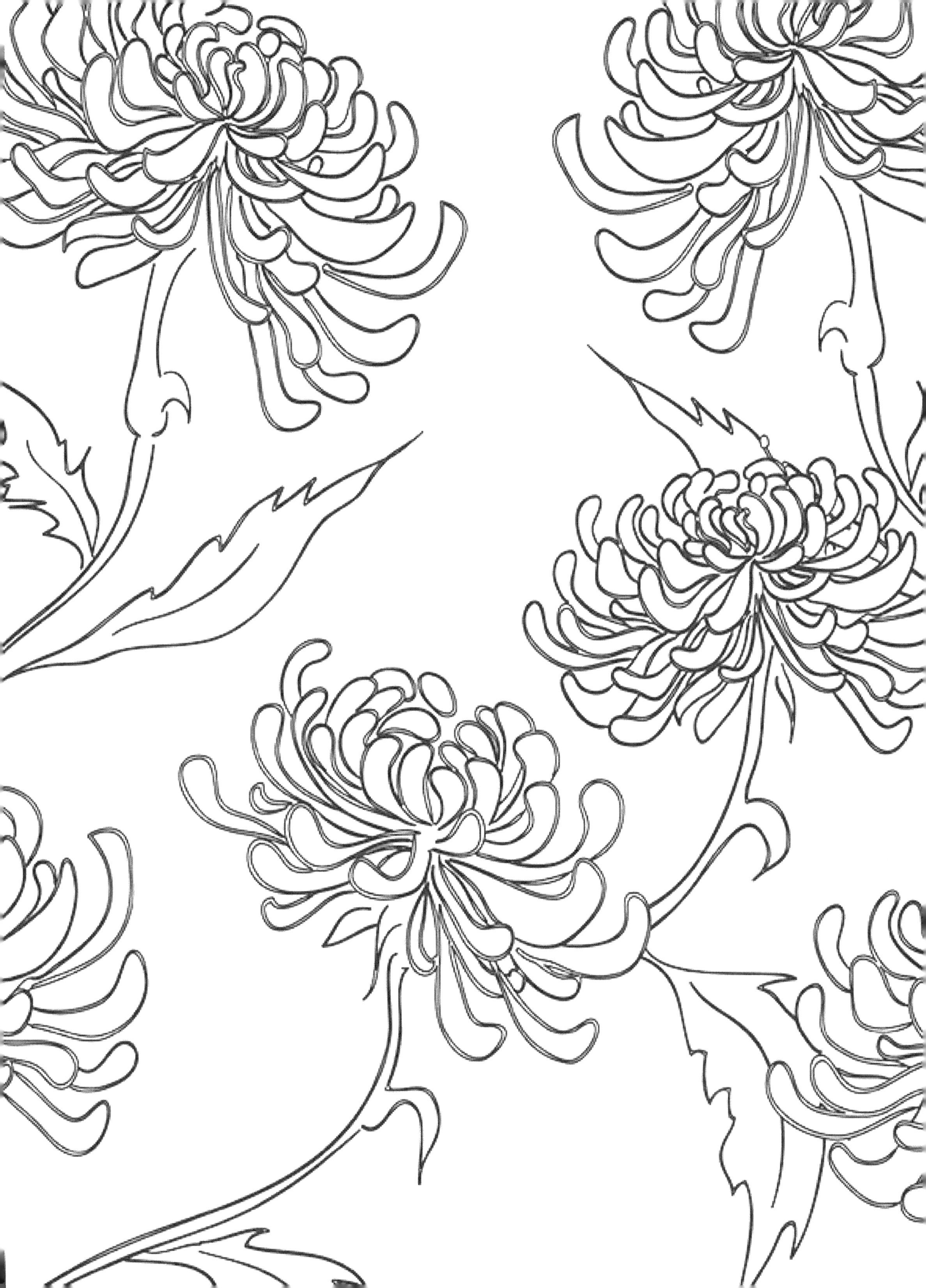

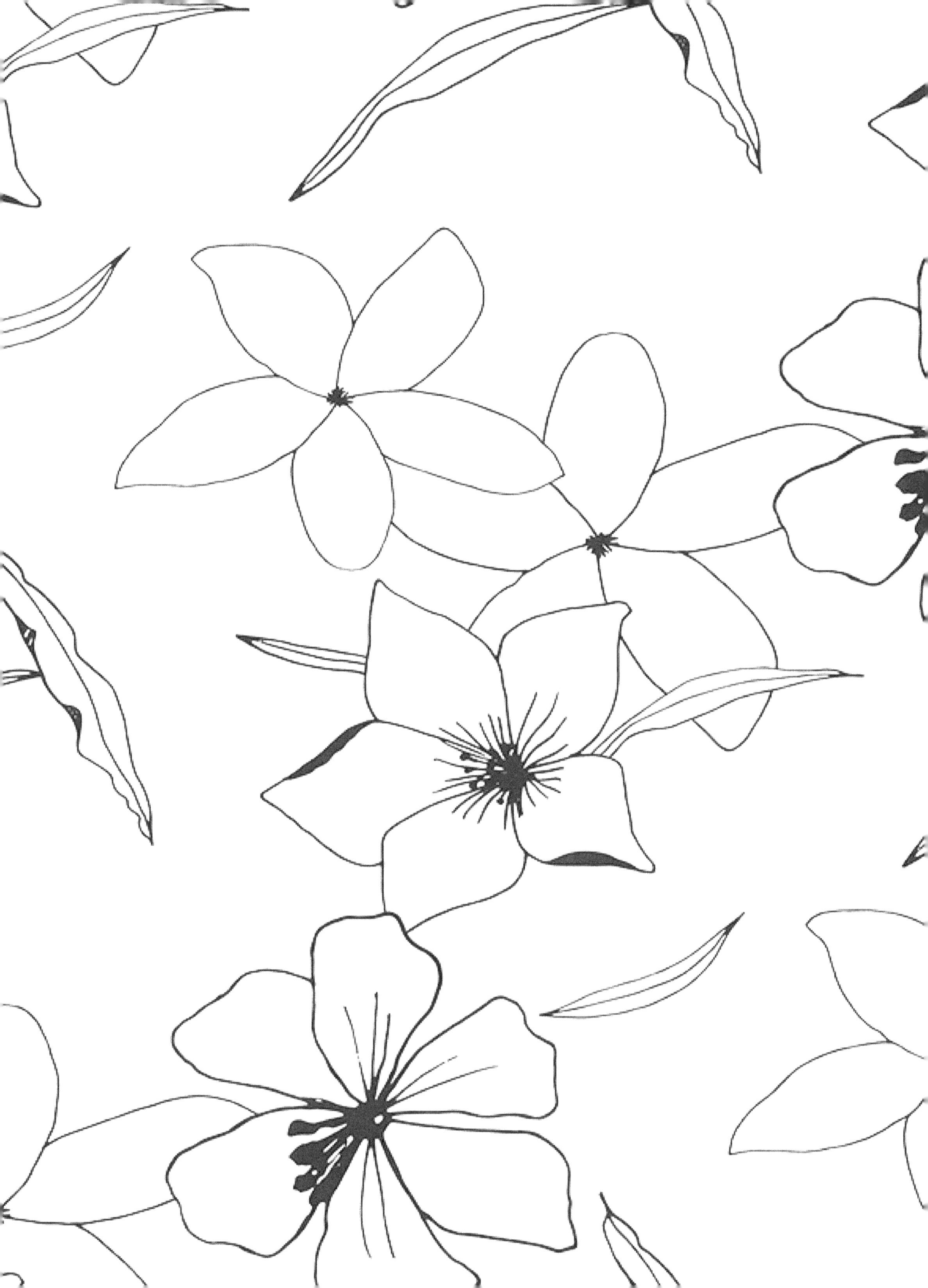

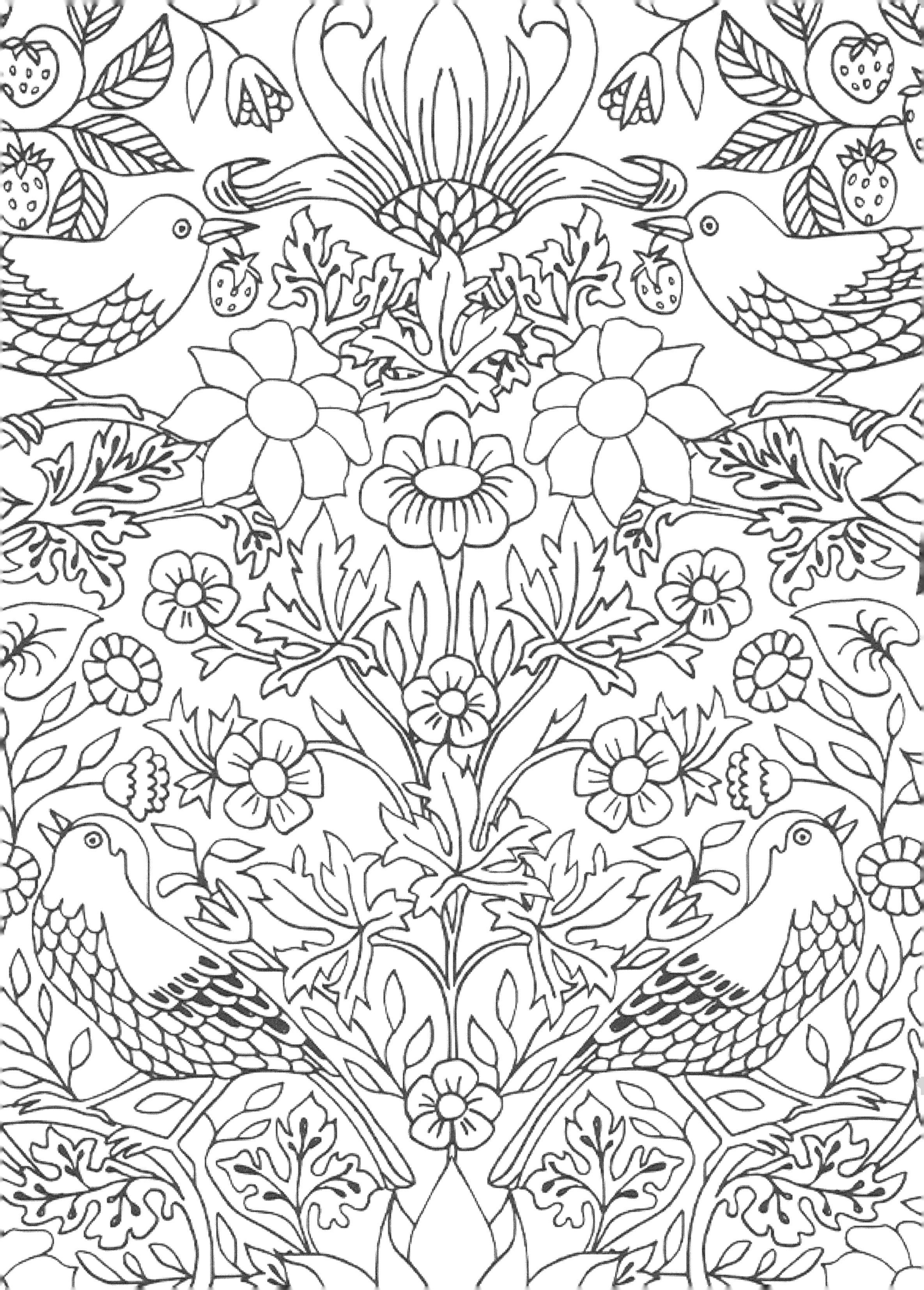

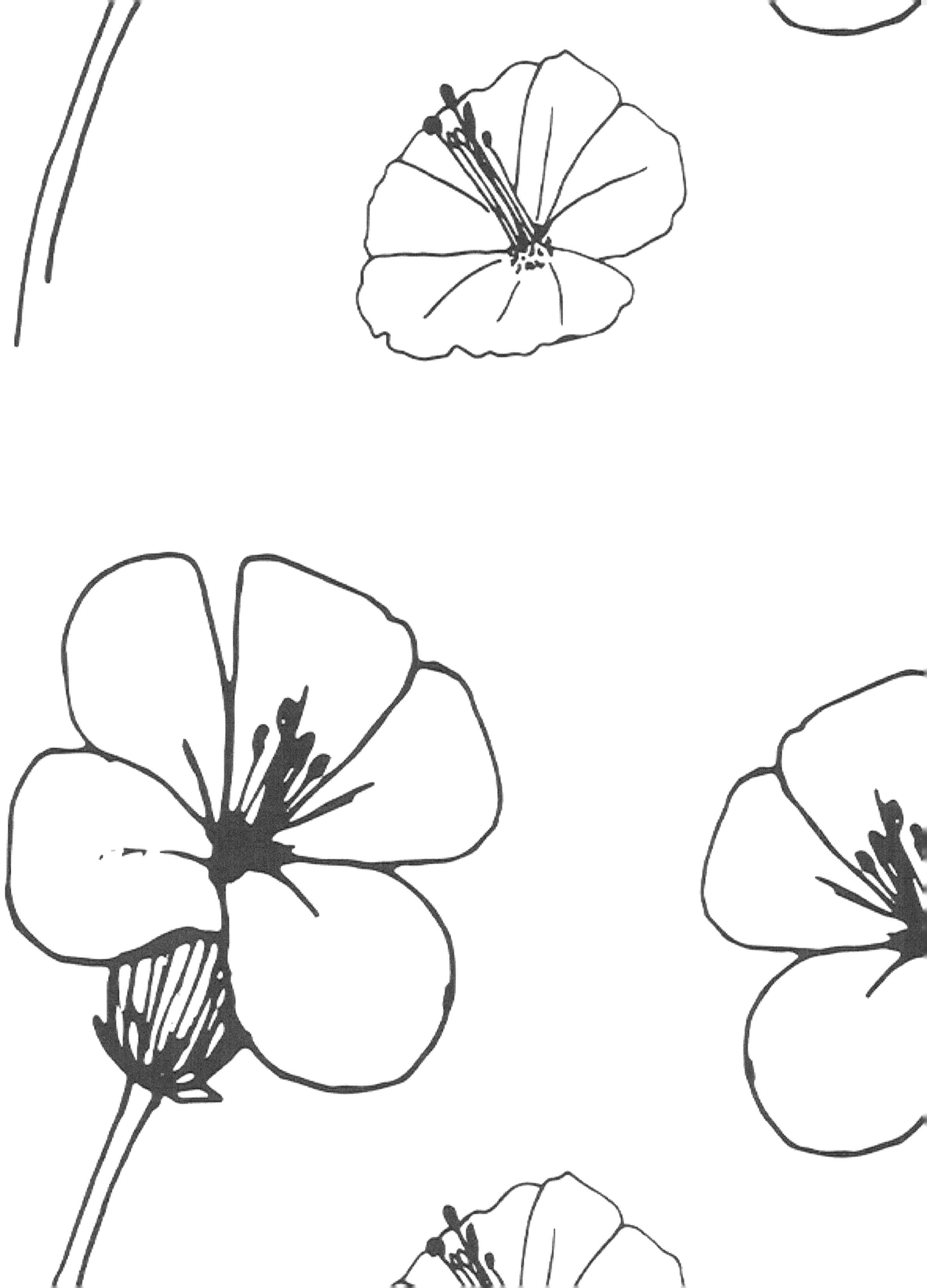

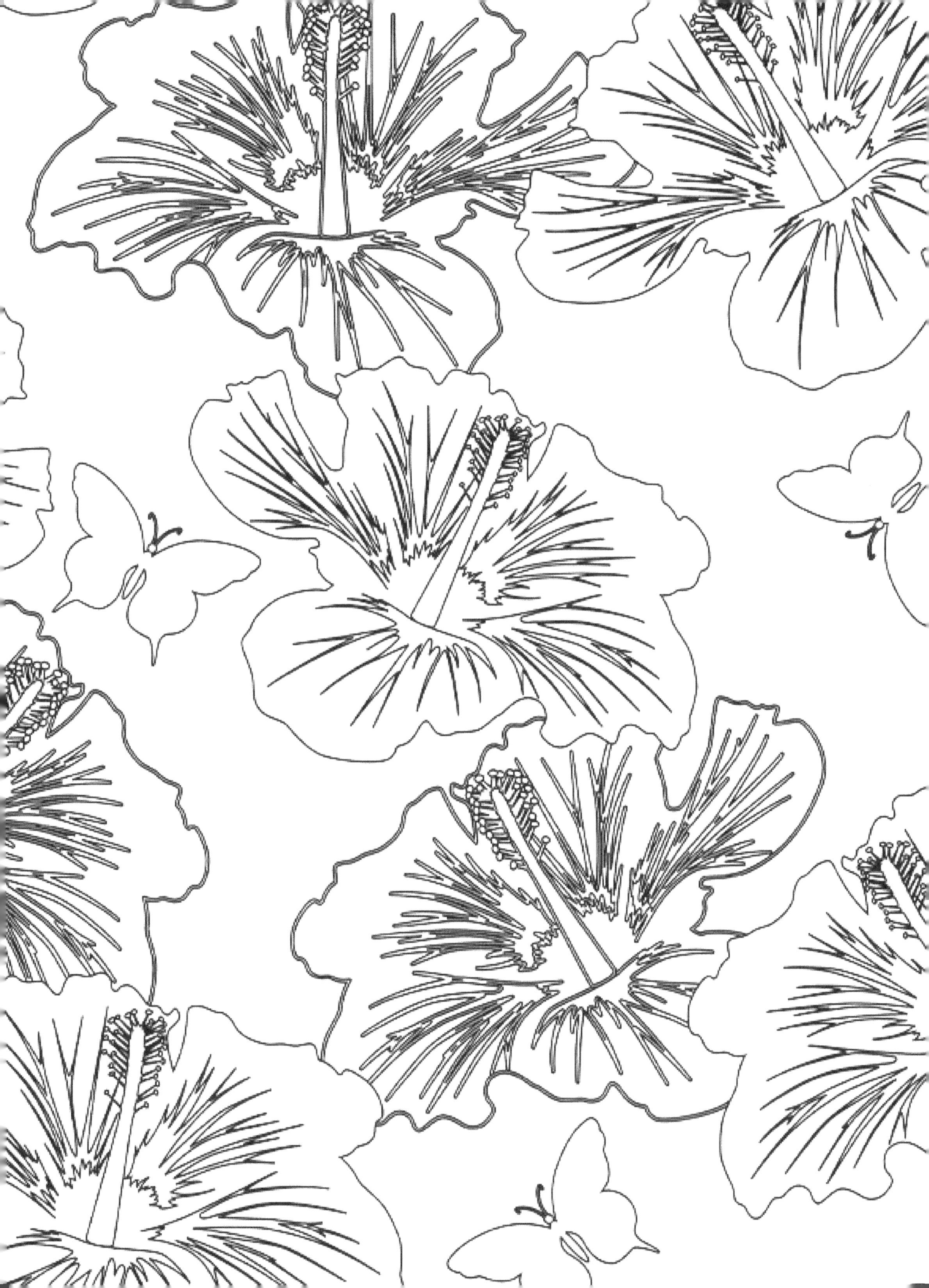

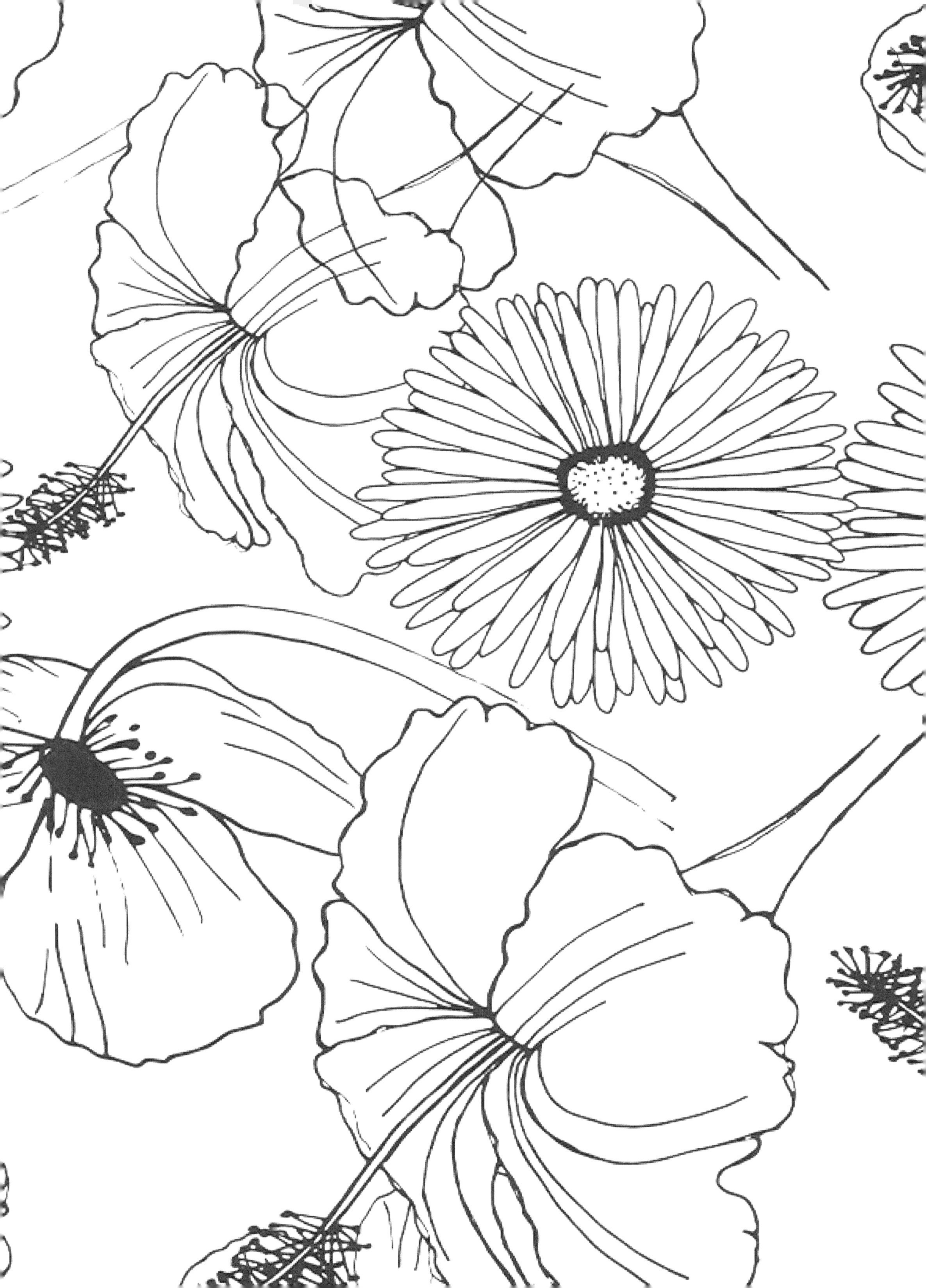

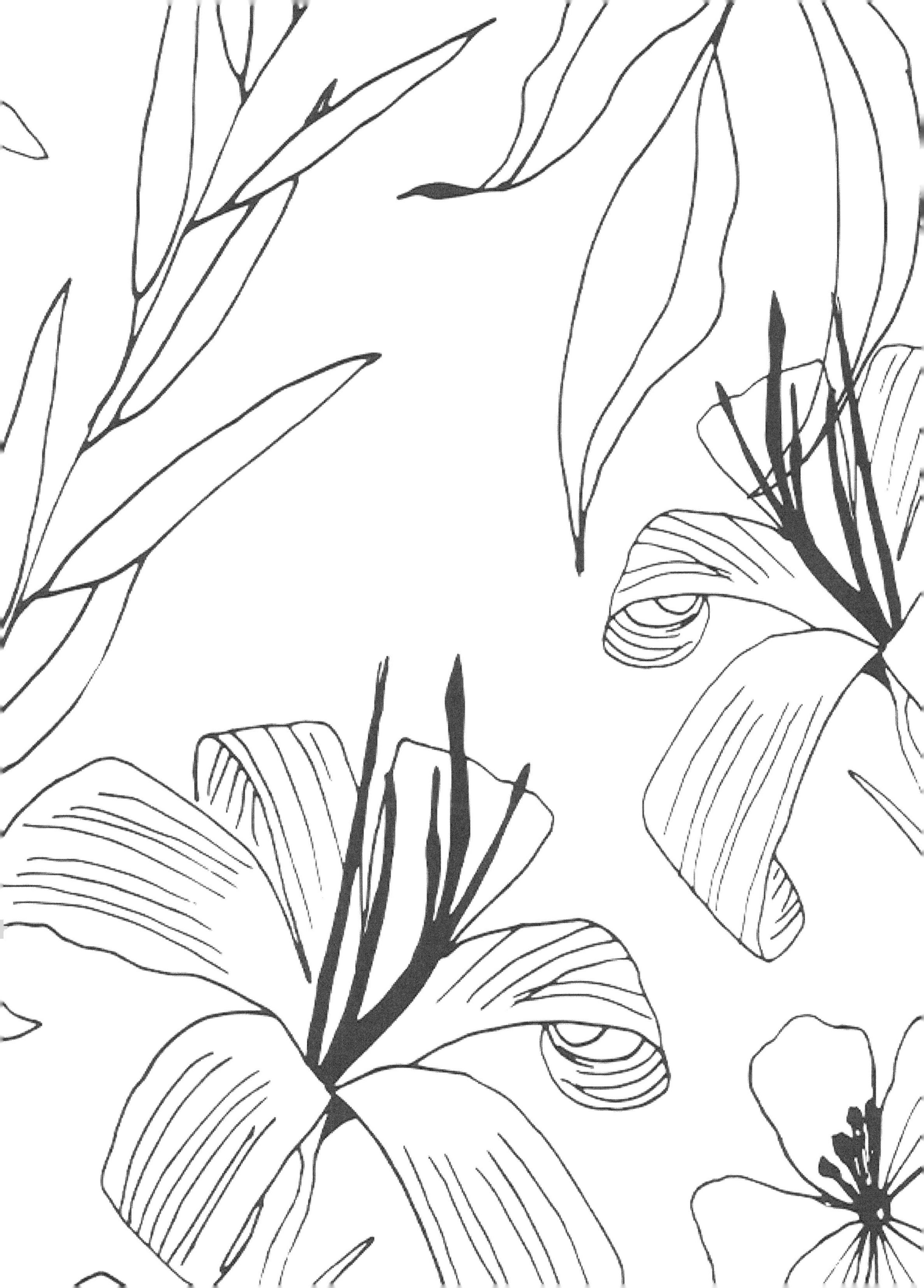

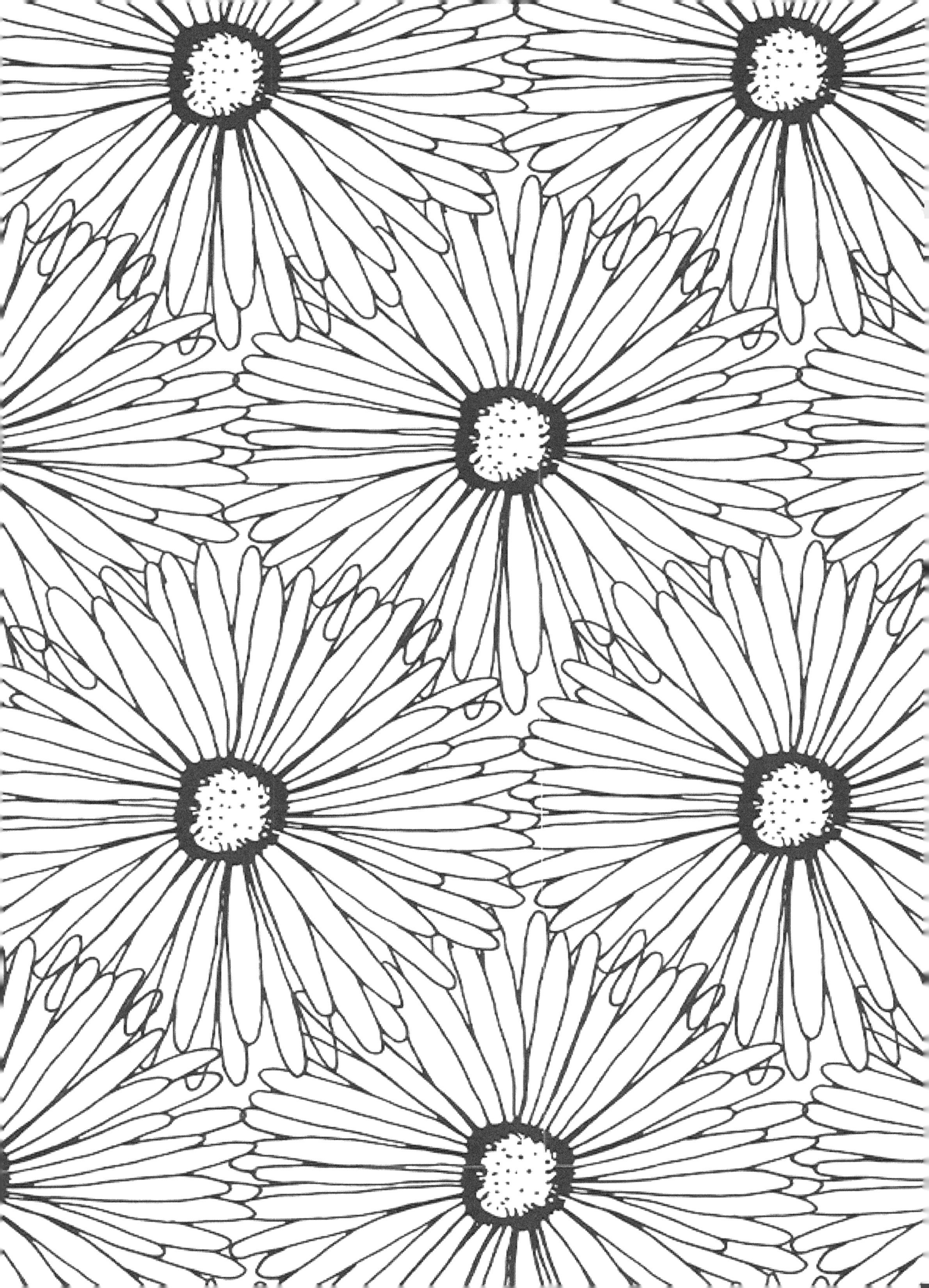

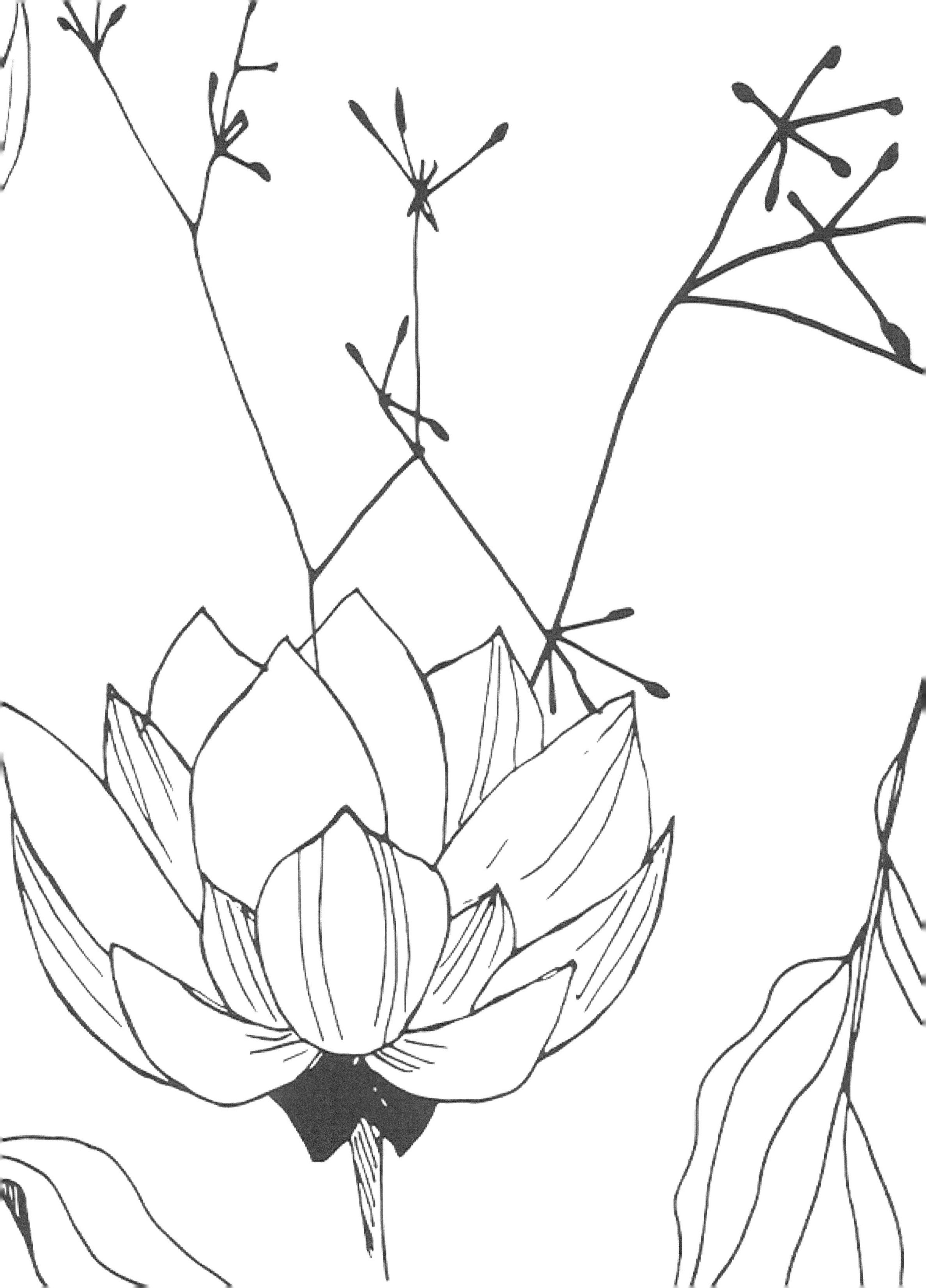

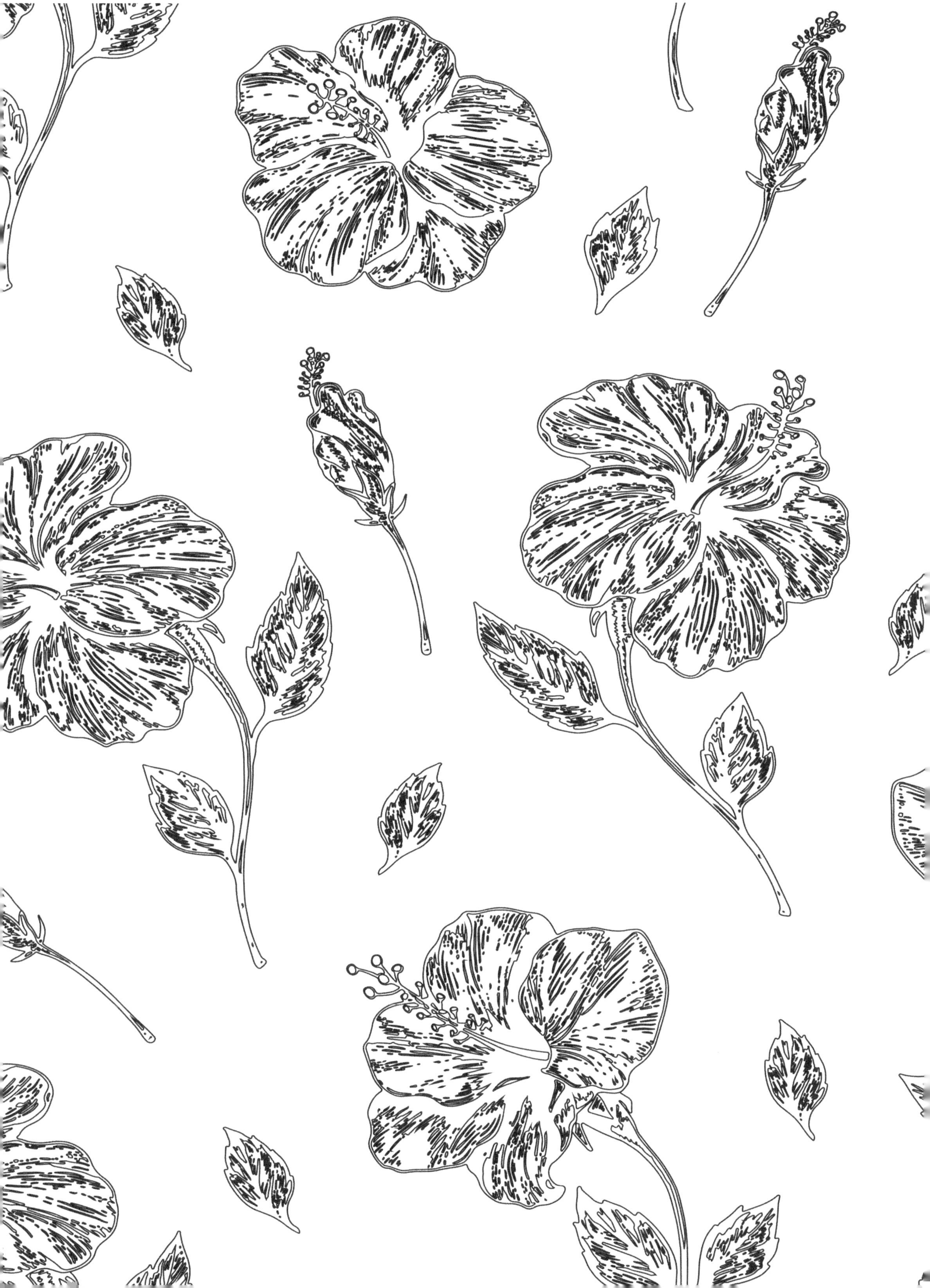

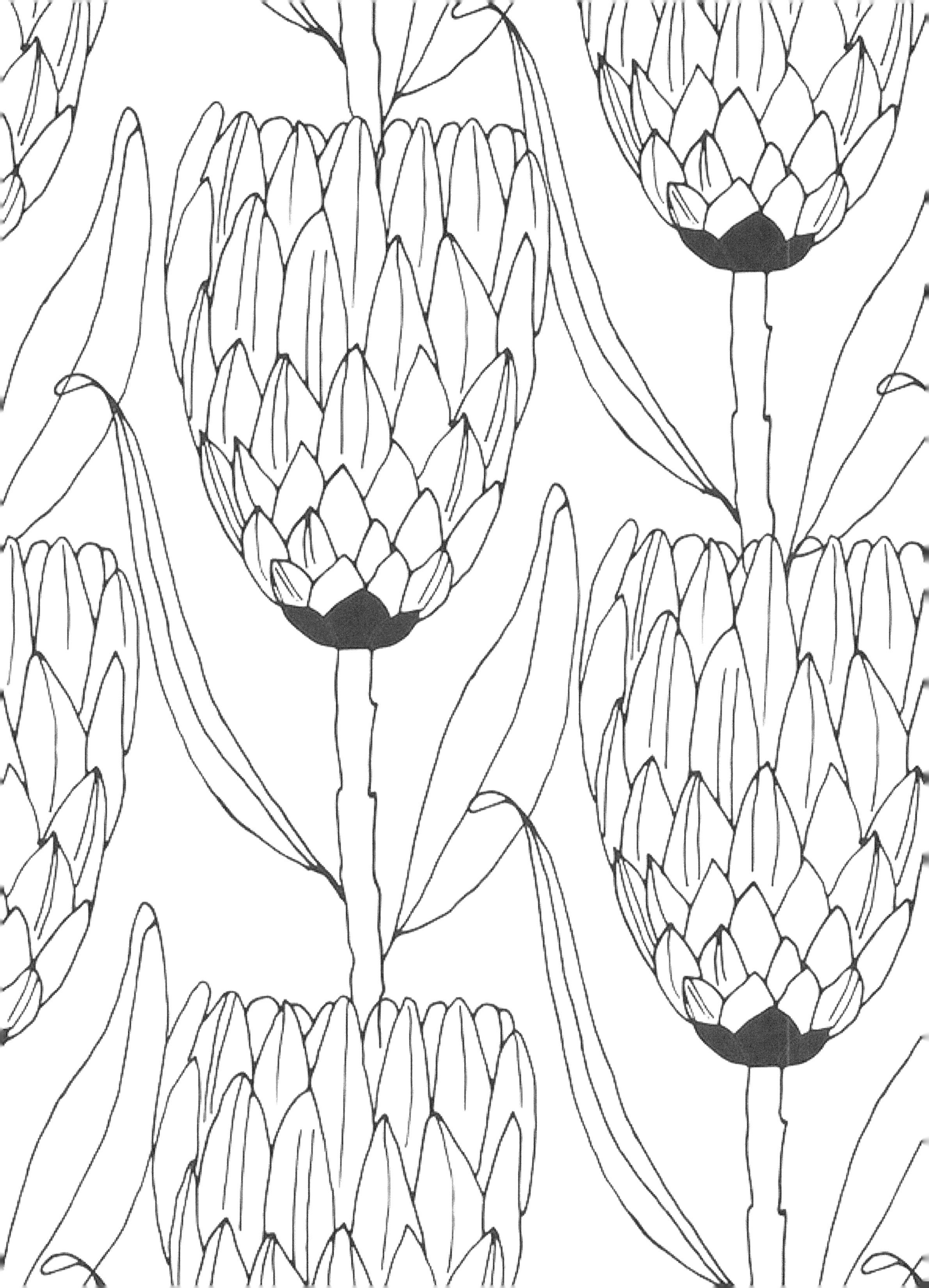

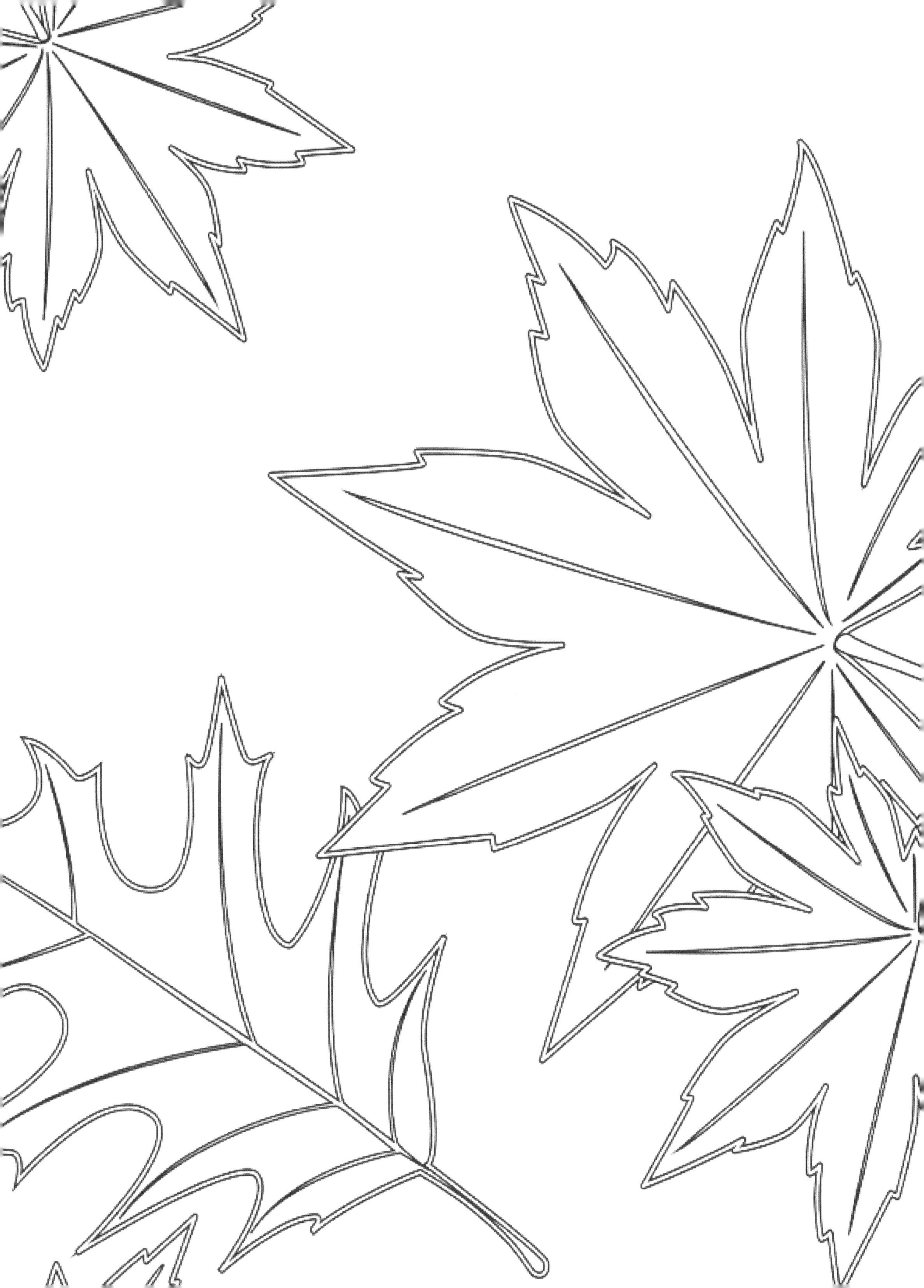

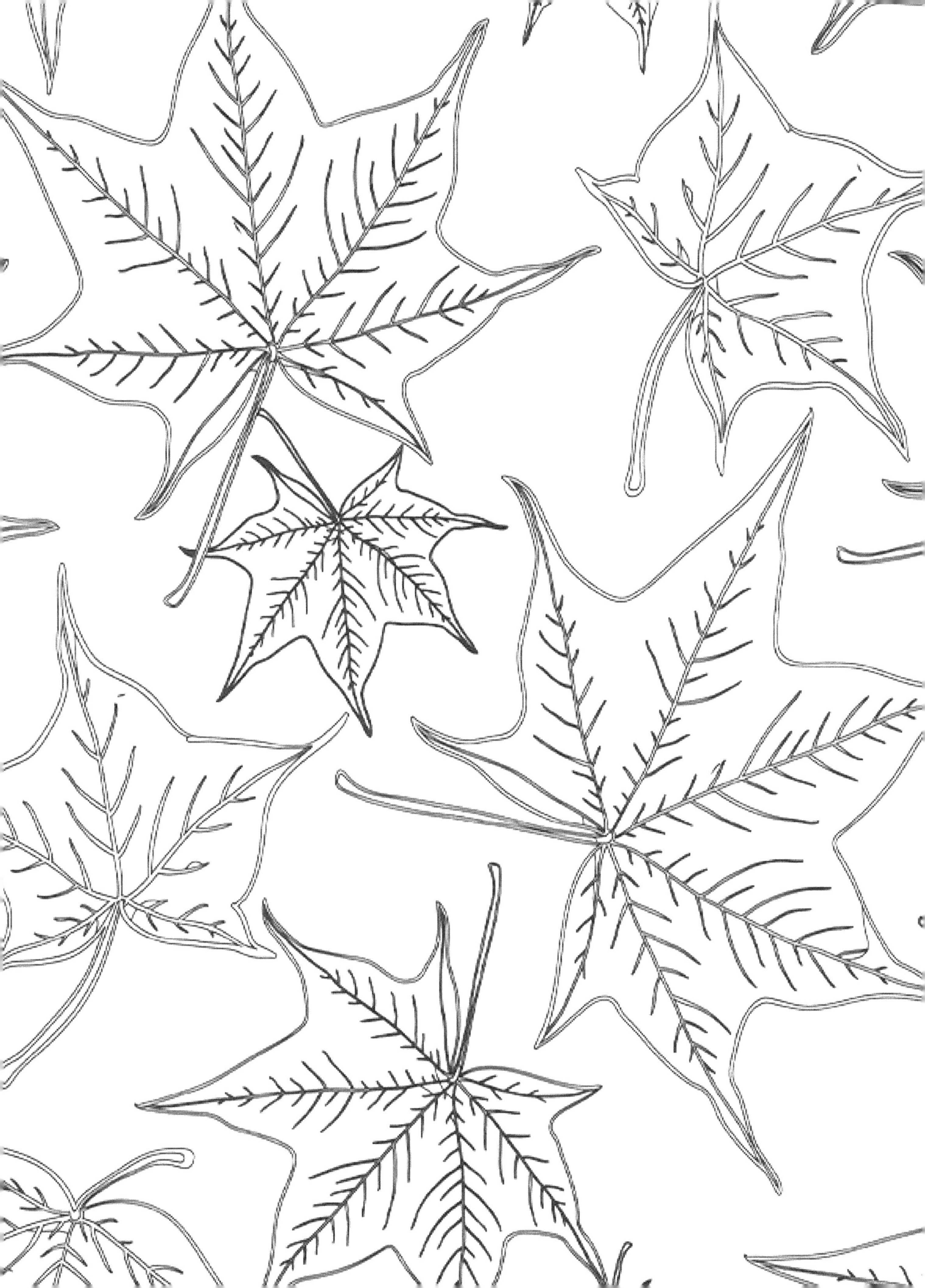

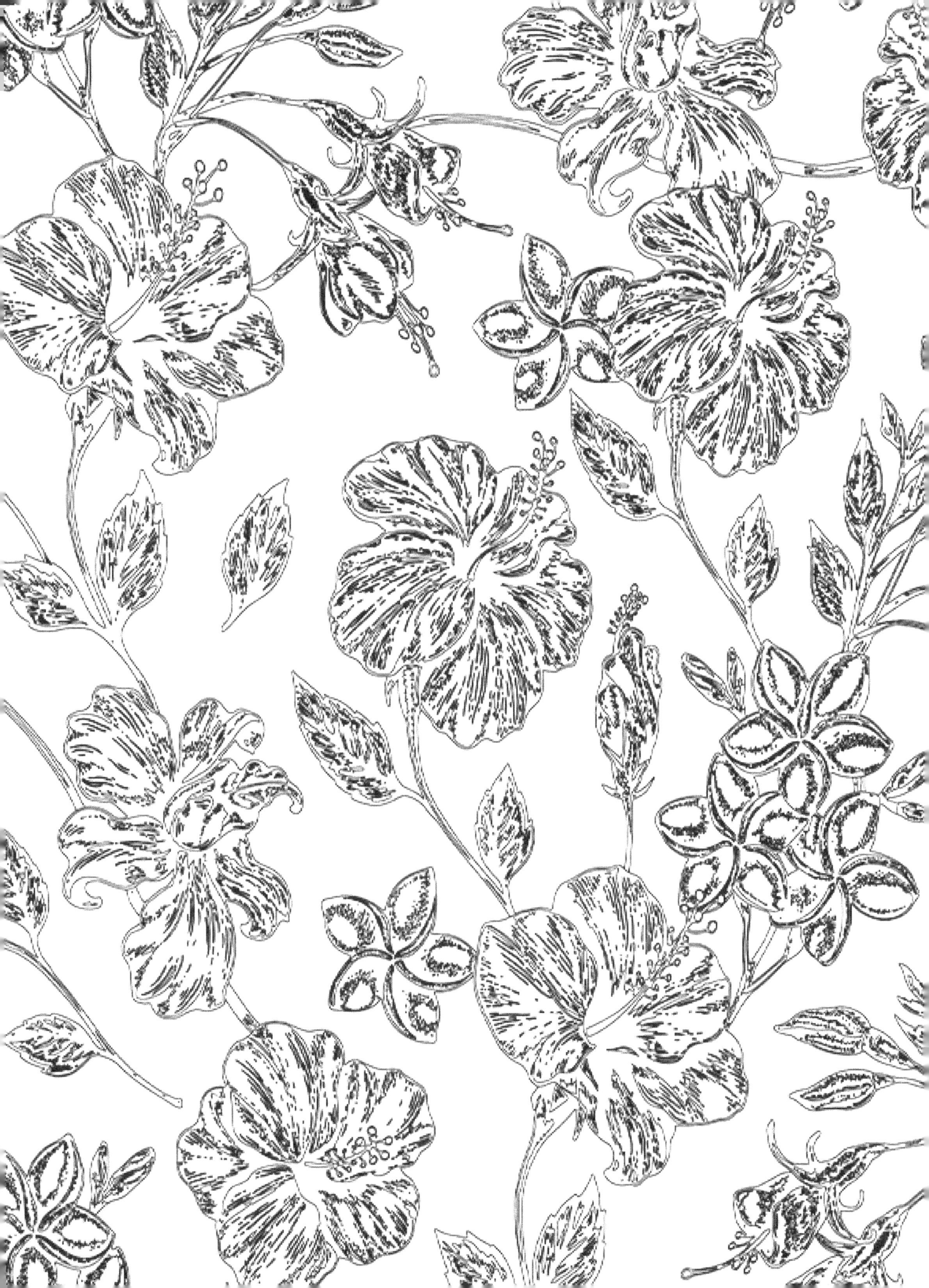

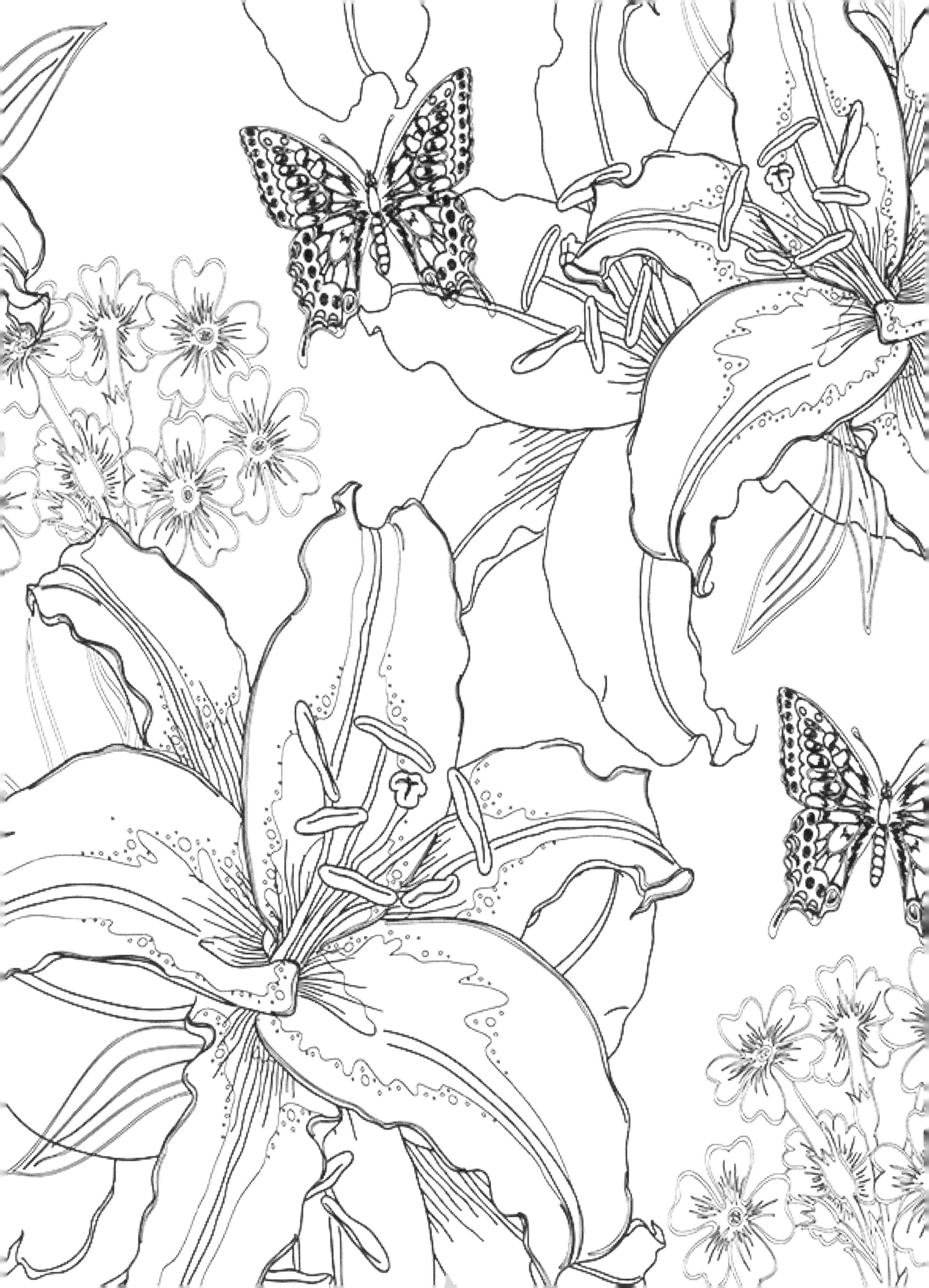

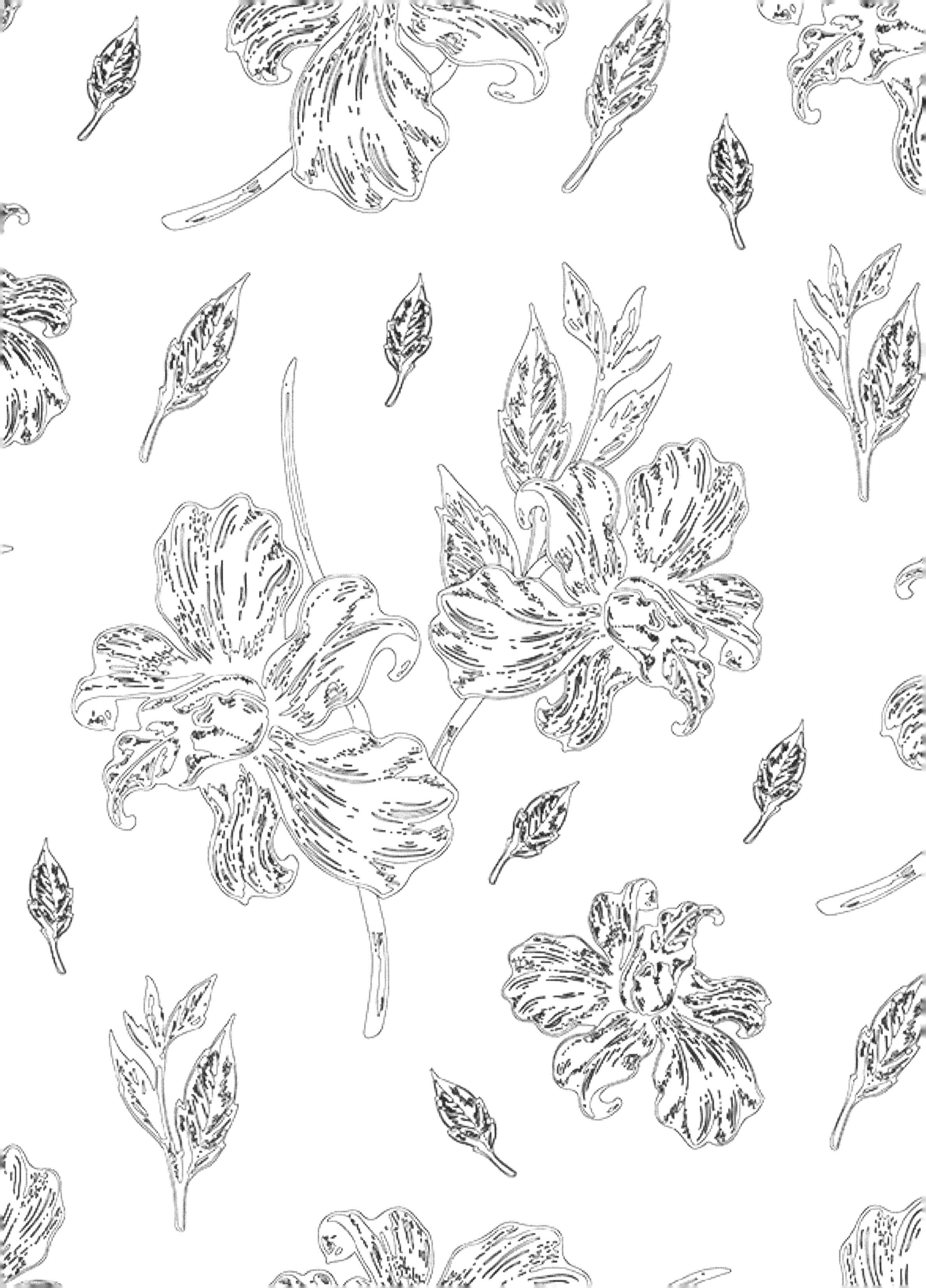

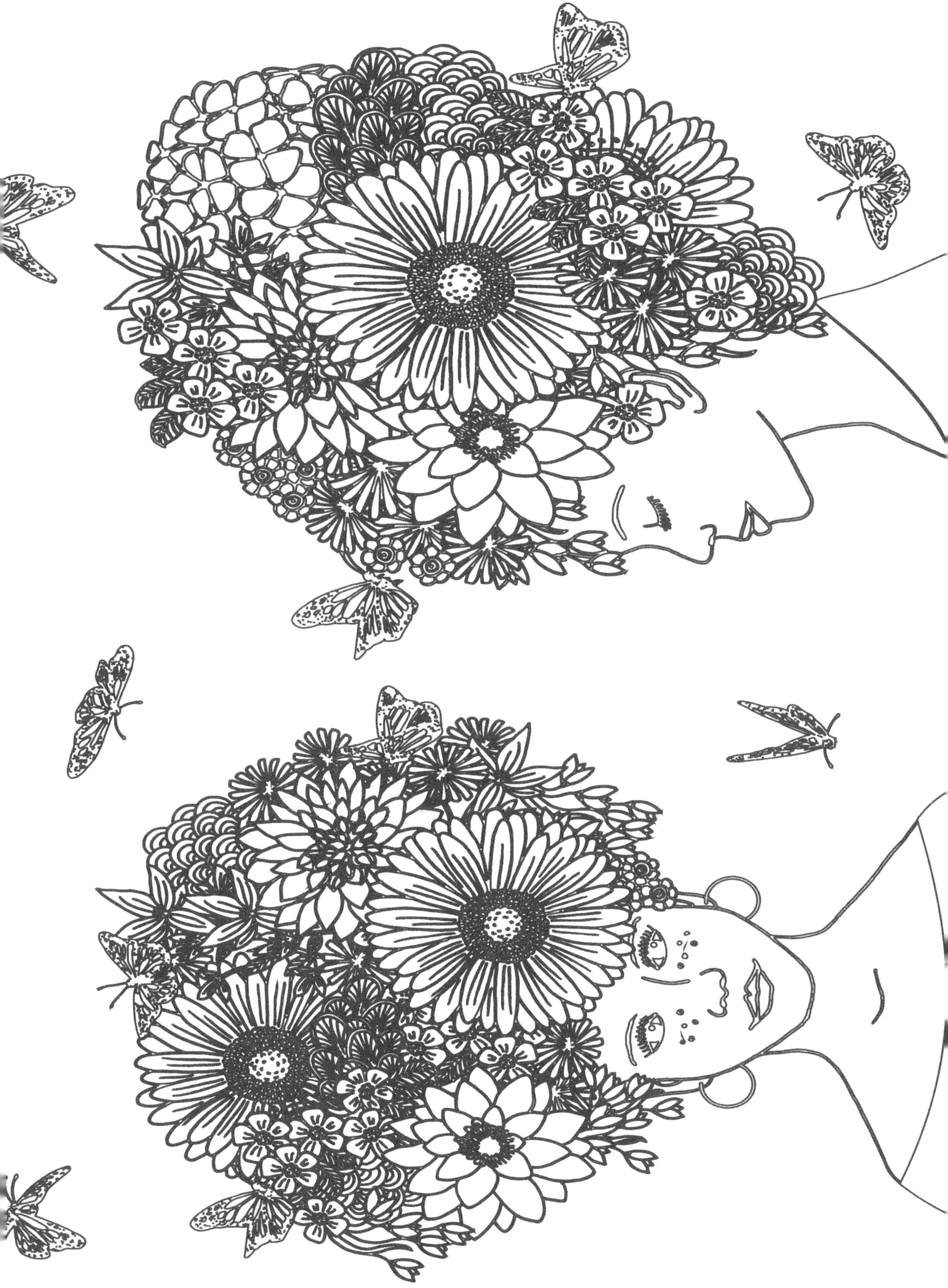

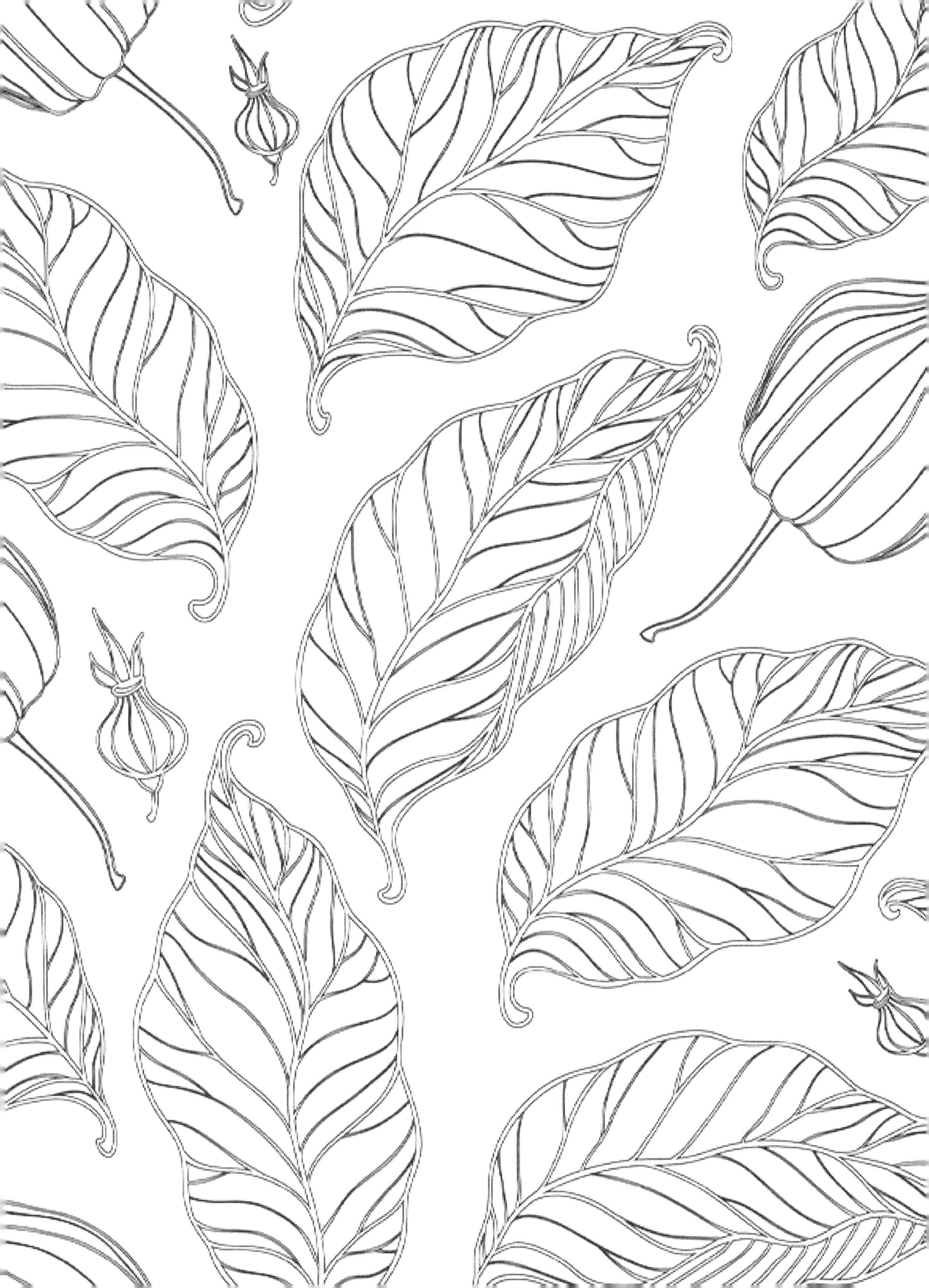